MW01223693

The Isle of Is

A GUIDE TO AWAKENING

CAROLINE COTTOM

THOM CRONKHITE

The Center Within
Koro Island, Fiji

USP Library Cataloguing-in-Publication Data
Cottom, Caroline
    The isle of is : a guide to awakening / Caroline Cottom, Thom Cronkhite.
Koro, Fiji : The Center Within.
    192 p. ; 23 cm
    ISBN 978-982-98004-1-1
1. Spirituality 2. Spiritual life 3. Enlightenment 4. Awakening – Christianity.
I. Cronkhite, Thom
BL476.C67 2006
        291.4

Copyright © 2006 Caroline Dare Cottom and Thomas Arden Cronkhite.
All Rights Reserved.

Caroline Dare Cottom and Thomas Arden Cronkhite assert their moral right to be identified as the authors of this work.

First published in 2006 by The Center Within, Waisali Village, Koro Island, Fiji Islands.

Design, artwork, and project management by Streamline Creative Ltd, Auckland, New Zealand. Cover design by Heather Lee. Front cover illustration and map by Jeffrey K. Bedrick. Ring of keys illustration by Myah Thormod.

Printed in China through Colorcraft Ltd, Hong Kong.

No part of this publication may be reproduced, stored in a retrieval system, or transmitted in any form or by any manner or means without written permission from the publisher.

For
all passengers
who find themselves
ready to disembark

All ashore
that's
going ashore

Acknowledgements

The kindness and generosity of David and Elsa Miller have made the publication of this book possible. Their dedication to the well-being of all sentient beings goes far beyond this project. We are also deeply grateful for the faith, trust, and encouragement we have received through the generous support of Melinda B. Scrivner over the years. May these blessings be bestowed upon everyone who picks up this book.

For the teachings themselves, we are deeply grateful to the spiritual masters who have preceded us: Gautama Buddha, Jesus, Jelaluddin Rumi, Maharishi Mahesh Yogi, Ramana Maharshi, Ram Dass, Eckhart Tolle, and others. We honor the traditions they represent, as well as those peoples who have held high the lamp of Truth throughout humanity's time on Earth.

We have been divinely inspired to share these teachings with the world, in order that we might provide greater understanding for the world's evolving spiritual awareness. For inspiration to write *The Isle of Is,* we especially thank our families and all those who have contributed to our work with their presence and support – meditators, friends, online students, retreat participants, creativity and writing students, and individuals seeking spiritual guidance.

In 2003, the sacred energies of Koro Island, Fiji, drew us like a spiritual magnet to live, work, and offer our teachings from the South Pacific. In this pristine and harmonious environment, Divine Presence shows itself readily. Here, *The Isle of Is* came to fruition.

We thank Tim Chamberlain at Streamline Creative, and Barbara Shine, for helping to bring clarity to our words, so that our message might find an even wider audience. We honor Jeff Bedrick, whose glorious art graces the cover and map; and Myah Thormod, whose drawing of keys helps guide the reader to the sacred sites of Is.

Blessings to All. May you come to the understanding that *You are the Blessing*.

Legend

Opening to Timeless Truth

The book you hold in your hands is based on wisdom that humans have known about for a very long time – sacred knowledge that is found among indigenous peoples throughout the world and captured in many ancient texts. This wisdom reveals the essence of Spirit and how it interweaves with all creation. By "Spirit" we mean the all-powerful, omnipresent energy of love that pervades all matter and space. Throughout the book, we use the terms Spirit, God, Being, Presence, and Divine Presence interchangeably to refer to that energy.

Drawing on this sacred wisdom, *The Isle of Is* explores the possibility of living awakened: so aware of Spirit both within and outside of one's self that one experiences constant peace, joy, and connection to all things. We use the word "awakened" rather than "enlightened" because the latter suggests seeking and attaining, whereas "awakened" refers to discovering what is already there. By undertaking the journey set forth in this book, you will use the tools described and develop the understandings that will assist you in uncovering that state of Being where peace and joy already exist, throughout time and space.

Written as a magical parable, *The Isle of Is* invites your senses and spirit to join your mind on this adventure. This is key to the process of awakening, for it is more than the mind that awakens. Our heart, our sensory body, and our spirit or soul also recognize and reclaim the state of peacefulness and joy. It is through the body and the senses that we receive the experience of awakening; they are the window for the divine experience that flows into our hearts, and back out again into the world.

This state of peacefulness and joy occurs when we turn our awareness totally to God and Nature. A common thread among indigenous peoples at the highest points of their cultures is that they have lived in accord with Nature. Pacific Islanders, Maori, Australian Aborigines, indigenous Africans, Incans, Mayans, other Native Americans, ancient Celts, and others have shared the myth and the understanding that they are chosen guardians of the territory they inhabit. Their daily activities and their relationship with Nature are continuous reminders of their connection to Spirit. In these cultures, medicine men and women, holy men, and shamans foster the link between their people's humanness and their divinity.

Ancient texts and revered spiritual teachers tell us that we are indeed divine. Jesus speaks of the kingdom of God within. Sufi poet and mystic Jelaluddin Rumi invites us to acknowledge the Presence that is in and around us. In the Agamas, Shiva tells his divine spouse and offspring that the greatest spiritual practice is to acknowledge one's self as the primordial source. The Upanishads, Agamas, and Vedas (sacred texts of India); teachings of the Tao; Karma Dharma Buddhist teachings; the true teachings of Jesus; the Kabbalah; and Sufist writings of Rumi and Hafiz – all speak of moving beyond the limits that we and society have imposed, to open ourselves to the limitless expansion of Divine Presence that we are.

These indigenous peoples and ancient texts are keepers of a sacred truth: namely, that we are one with everything. We, the rocks, the mighty redwoods, and the antelopes are all made of the same spiritual essence. The same divine energy that flows through dolphins and stars also flows through us. Whether or not you believe that you are divine, *The Isle of Is* offers you the opportunity to explore the validity of this idea for yourself. The book is deeply experiential, inviting you to tap your own inner knowing by entering into silence and scribing your personal wisdom.

While the sacred teachings in this book are timeless, most of humanity has only now become ready to listen. Predicted by the Mayan calendar; astrologers of ancient Greece, Phoenicia, and Egypt; Jewish astrologers; the Hopi Nation; Buddhist philosophers; and the East Indian cosmology of the yugas, the era of illumination is upon us. It is the Golden Age, the Age of Aquarius, when humankind is more open to spiritual understanding and truth than ever before. The writings and teachings of modern-day spiritual teachers Maharishi Mahesh Yogi, Ramana Maharshi, Eckhart Tolle, David Hawkins, and others reflect this increased consciousness. It is a remarkable era, one in which humanity as a whole has come into a place of "integrity," as defined by David Hawkins in *The Eye of the I* – the first time we are at the point where our consciousness has advanced to the level where we are able to comprehend truth.

In days of old, only priests, shamans, and other holy men were privy to the sacred texts. This was true among many indigenous peoples as well; for example, the Ring of Knowledge in Hopi, Aztec, Maori, and other cultures referred to knowledge that was available for only a select few. By contrast, thousands of ordinary men and women are discovering the process of awakening. Indeed, you do not need to be a student of theology, a shaman, or a spiritual adept in order to be transformed by what this book offers.

The Isle of Is describes 11 keys based on this wisdom, reflected in the 11 aspects that make up the Sacred Realm. We introduce the keys in the context of a parable – a teaching story – of a spiritual traveler on the paradisiacal Island of Is. As the traveler explores the island, guided by Nature, Spirit, and his or her own intuition, the ancient wisdom is revealed. Nature's creatures come alive in the book, in the tradition of many indigenous peoples, shamans, and the folklore of numerous ancient cultures. This is not just fanciful story-telling. The authors' perception and experience is that Nature – Mother Earth – Spirit – is communicating with us all the time through trees, spiders, ocean waves, and stones.

Recent advances in science and philosophy substantiate the truths contained here, showing us how our minds really operate. Western science is just now coming to understand the power of our perceptions and mental images to limit – or enlarge – our lives. Molecular biologists, for example, are discovering that our perceptions, not our genes, determine our biology. At the same time, neuroscientists have substantiated that the brain is not in charge, demonstrating at a cellular level how our emotions transform our bodies and create our health.

During the past two decades of cognitive research, scientists have learned that, contrary to what we once thought, our mind is embodied; that is, based in our senses. What we *think* grows out of our experience in a human body. We have concepts of "front" and "back," for example, because our eyes are on the front of our heads. If we had eyes all around, our concepts about location and position would be radically different. Similarly, if we were amphibious – able to breathe, hear, and see under water – we might view emotions and thoughts as fluid and weightless instead of complex or heavy. Rather than the long-taught Western concept "I think, therefore I am," science is now proving that "I am, therefore I think" is much closer to the truth.

Furthermore, our fundamental concepts about life, morality, affection, the mind, time, and much more are based in metaphors (sensory images) that control our perceptions. Of particular interest is the controlling life metaphor, an internalized image that shapes and limits the kind of life we live. Usually hidden from our awareness, these images underlie our beliefs and are far more powerful. The metaphor "life is a struggle," for example, limits one's life experience to difficulty and conflict; any experience that does not align with the metaphor is rejected. A life metaphor of "life is a search," another metaphor prevalent in today's world, relegates one to a life of searching without really finding.

Thousands of life metaphors exist – some common, some delightfully unique. They operate sub-consciously, and they operate consistently across humanity. No one is exempt. Unless people become aware of their metaphors on a conscious level and replace them with others that affirm their true nature, they are unlikely to be free of the metaphors' influence on their lives.

Today's scientists and philosophers, like the ancient sages before them, are pointing to this truth: Life is not as limited as we may have thought. Indeed, it is our perceptions that keep us from entertaining the idea that we could live a life of constant peace, joy, and connection to everything. Many people simply do not believe it is possible. Even some religious leaders tell us that it will require eons and eons of struggle and suffering before we are able to live an awakened life. But this too is a perception – a belief – and a drastically limiting one at that. As a belief, it can be changed.

The Isle of Is provides a significant departure from the ways that awakening and enlightenment have been taught before. Secret societies, hierarchy, severe discipline, austerities, isolation, and extreme seriousness are typical of these approaches. By contrast, we use parables, real-life stories, sensory images, and humor in the tradition of Jesus, the Buddha, Jelaluddin Rumi, the Baal Shem Tov, and other spiritual masters. Tools unique to the age in which we live, fresh and engaging material, and a light-hearted, joyful approach allow people from all walks of life to become open to possibilities they never considered within their reach.

This book is your invitation to explore that ground. The ferry to Sacred Island awaits you. The indigenous peoples, the ancient ones, and the holy mothers and fathers all stand before you, arms outstretched.

'Welcome,' they say. 'Welcome to the Island of Is.'

1 | *Ferry to Sacred Island*

What lies behind ye and what lies before ye
are tiny matters, compared to what lies within ye.

Ralph Waldo Emerson

We sit in the prow of a boat that ferries people back and forth across a wide sea, having left the known shore just moments before. Our ticket is stuffed in our pocket, following a last-minute decision to hop on board. It was Anna, an old friend, who took this trip recently, and when she came home, a light shone on her face that we had not seen on anyone.

The light did not fade, and we were entranced. 'Where did you go? And what was it like?' we asked.

'I have no words to describe the experience,' she said, 'except to tell you this: It is the most beautiful place, an island set in the bluest ocean you have ever seen, and what exists there is a serenity you have probably never felt. Go. You will not regret a single minute of the trip.'

And here we are, the only passenger, and treated like royalty by a ferryman with ruddy cheeks, marine-blue eyes, and waves of curly white hair. We brought a knapsack for the few clothes we will need; Anna has assured us that everything else will be taken care of. So far, she is right. Once we were underway, the ferryman gave us nourishment and assured us of a wondrous experience. He congratulated us for our decision to visit the Sacred Realm.

The boat rocks gently on the open sea, its sails billowing, and terns and black-bellied petrels swoop near the prow, skimming the waves. They seem to commune with us, as they lift on the air currents and splash into the sea as though performing for an audience.

'Aye, they are greeting ye,' says the ferryman. 'They recognize ye for the Divine Presence that ye are.'

They recognize ye for the Divine Presence that ye are.

We laugh. Our work back home has been stressful, and our life sometimes feels overwhelming. Divine Presence, indeed!

But the ferryman nods in understanding, as though he has heard our thoughts. 'Life sometimes gets the better of ye, does it?' he says.

'Yes, it does.' We turn back to scan the horizon.

Ahead of us, an island has come into view: Rainforest covers the mountains, and the lush green trees spill down to a bone-white beach. We are mesmerized by the island's beauty and think out loud: 'The sun seems to bless this place.'

'Time to go ashore, dear friend,' says the ferryman, once we have drawn close to land. 'I will set anchor and row ye to shore.'

We set off for the beach in a tiny boat. There is a silence . . . and the sound of oars. While the ferryman rows, we look around, seeing no evidence of a resort or houses.

'Is there no place to stay?' we ask the ferryman.

'Everything will be taken care of,' he assures us, continuing to row. 'Do not concern yourself about anything. Follow your intuition and all will be well.'

As we near the shore, he bends to pull something from under his seat. 'Almost forgot your tools. Ye will likely need these.' With eyes gleaming, he hands us a leather cylinder with a brass clasp and a leather strap.

'Our tools?' The cylinder looks like an arrow quiver. For a moment we are afraid. Will we have to hunt our own food?

'Instructions included. Best to open it when ye get ashore. But, here, I'll trade ye; hand me that knapsack, ye won't be needing it any more.'

Before we can protest, he takes the knapsack and holds out his hand to help us get out of the boat and into the shallow water. Smiling broadly, he begins to row the tiny boat back to the ferry.

Glancing at the larger boat, we notice letters painted on the side that we had not seen before: **E.Satva**. The boat E. Satva? It must have some hidden meaning for the ferryman.

We realize we don't have a clue as to what we are to do next.

The beach stretches for a couple of miles on either side of our landing point. There are no buildings in sight, no roads or paths, no footprints. Only trees and beach. Surely others have come before us? We don't know where we are, or who we are, for that matter! We feel different, strange – not in a bad way – but we are wondering what has led us to this place.

And the cylinder – what is this? Once on the sand, we unhook the clasp. The cylinder is hinged at the midpoint and opens into two halves. Rolled inside is a pad of blank paper, and tucked into one of the halves are a pen and inkwell. The inkwell is labeled, *Silence of Mind*. A separate sheet of paper reads:

Instructions

These are your tools: The pen shall be your **Wand**
for 'the write of passage' that will take you back and forth
to the Sacred Realm. The paper, of course, you will write on.
The inkwell signifies the **Well**, which is the silence within.
'The way in is the way out.'

When instructed, the two tools will work together:
You will go to the **Well**, be in silence,
then you will pick up your **Wand**.
What did you discover in the **Well**?
What did you bring back?
You will begin to write . . .

'The way in is the way out' – enigmatic, to be sure. And when and where will we use these tools? We are becoming a bit anxious – no people, no houses, no path, no useful instructions. We need help.

Anna's face comes to mind, with its peaceful glow. 'No worries,' she says. 'Gather your things and walk down the beach to your right, following the shore.'

We glance right, at what seems to be an empty beach. 'Okay,' we think, 'what do we have to lose?' Resigned, we sling the cylinder over our shoulder and set off in that direction.

It is a beach, after all, so we take off our shoes and walk at the water's edge, feeling the sand ooze between our toes. Above us, the sky is the clearest blue, and the clouds are small white and peach puffs that seem to go lightly on their way. We are mesmerized by such peace, such beauty. This is a far cry from our life back home.

After a few minutes we spot something near the line of trees – a roll of paper, perhaps – no, a parchment. And a ring . . . a ring of keys!

The roll of parchment stands upright in the sand, as though someone had stuck it there just moments before. The keys are arranged in a circle. Someone has evidently taken great care in setting them out. We pick up the ring to examine the keys; they are weighty and appear to be made of gold. Each is carved with an image from Nature – ocean, waterfall, mountain, stream.

Replacing the keys on the sand, we unroll the parchment to find a map, an outline really, of an island called The Isle of Is, surrounded on all sides by the Ocean of Being.

The Island of Is! We've heard stories of this place. It is a fabled place described by sages, mystics, philosophers, and poets of all time. A veritable Garden of Eden. The mythical island of Avalon. Sukhavati – the place of bliss, land of the gods. How could we be so lucky as to find ourselves on this island?

It was Anna, of course, who led us here. Or rather, what we saw in her face drew us here.

Again, we feel Anna's presence. We close our eyes and become quiet so that we can listen. Anna's voice resonates softly:

'Your purpose is to discover who you really are and to learn how to create a life of deep peace and joy. Each key holds sacred information that unlocks an aspect of the realm. All are inter-linked, like the magnetic forces that connect the stars. Go within, and trust, for you shall know what to do.'

Your purpose is to discover who you really are.

Anna's presence leaves as gently as it came.

We are alone again with the Island of Is and the sea, the great Ocean of Being.

Your Keys to the Realm

2 | *The Gate of Gratitude*

Leave your luggage at the gate;
*this **is** the entrance to the Sacred Realm.*

Saint Anonymous

In our hand are 11 keys with carved images – one shows a mountain peak; another, a cascading waterfall; still another, foam-tipped waves. We look closely at the images, trying to puzzle out where our journey will begin. Before us is dense mass of mangroves with prop roots that reach deep into the sand, and to both sides, a beach that stretches out of sight. We see no entrance to the forest, no path to the right or left. We study the ring of keys, thinking they may be numbered or encoded with symbols. But there are no numbers, no obvious codes.

To our astonishment, under our gaze one key begins to pulse with a golden glow. Almost imperceptibly, the key vibrates as though a low electric current were passing through it. Carved on its face is an arbor above a wooden gate. We glance around for an arbor but see none.

As we hold this key between thumb and forefinger, the vibration intensifies in magnitude, pulling us a short distance down the beach, as though beckoning us forward, and then toward the edge of the forest. We stop short at the line of trees, where mangrove roots create an impenetrable barrier. In their midst stand two large rain trees, entwined as if embracing. Their trunks twist around each other before their upper branches spread outward, two large umbrellas against the clear sky.

Suddenly the trees begin to rotate. Like partners in a dance, they separate, creating a space between them. Through the opening we see a dense forest and a grassy path. The key pulls us through the opening and onto the path. Excited and a little anxious, we turn to glance back at the beach. But as we do, the trees move again, slowly rotating back to their former position. They are entwined once more, and the beach has disappeared from sight.

Ahead of us the path vanishes into the forest, enticing us onward. Nature is indeed directing us onto this path. We don't know where the journey will take us, but there is no turning back. We heave a sigh, adjust our quiver, and set out.

Nature is indeed directing us onto this path.

The path meanders through rainforest, in the shade of ancient trees. Trumpet vines hanging from overhead branches dip and sway in the breeze. Ferns seem to explode from the crevices of tree trunks. On one tree, bright red hearts shoot from the trunk on tiny stems; on another, hundreds of vines plunge toward the soil like stalactites. The extraordinary beauty of this place lifts our spirits, and we find ourselves humming a tune, our steps becoming lighter.

We have entered a wondrous place, and for a moment we think we hear the voices of Nature spirits. Childhood stories of elves and fairies come to mind. Are we creating these thoughts, or is this a prelude to something else? Do we really hear fairylike giggling and tiny whispers? Do we really see the glimmer of things moving about quickly, and tiny eyes pointed in our direction?

Caught up in thoughts about what adventures might await us, we are surprised when the path curves suddenly to the right. We stop, for around the bend stands a wooden gate and an arbor laden with lush blooms. At the base of the gate grow gardenias and forget-me-nots, while bright pink and purple bougainvillea hang like grape clusters from the arbor arching above.

Our senses are intensely alive. The colors of the flowers vibrate against the rich greens of the forest. Sweet fragrances burst in the air as we draw near and reach out to touch the blossoms.

Above the gate, the flowers form letters, G – R – A – T . . . GRATITUDE. We look down at the key, but it contains no words. Then we remember the map of the Isle of Is.

We unroll the parchment, mystified that there is nothing on the map except an outline of the island. There must be some mistake! How will we find our way around the island if the map does not guide us?

Hoping to see faint lines or shapes, we hold the map overhead so that the light streaming through the branches strikes the parchment. To our amazement, the sun begins to etch into the parchment, slowly burning a sepia trail from the island's perimeter to its interior. As the path is etched, we hear a faint jingling sound, as though light particles are bouncing off one another. Then a drawing of a gate appears, and words form beside it:

The Gate of Gratitude

The sun has finished its etching, and the trail ends at the gate. We roll up the map and tuck it into our quiver.

Peering through the arch, we see a distant pool shimmering in the sun's light, surrounded by a jeweled forest. Birds and flowers adorn the trees with colors we've never seen before. The birds tweet and chirp as they flit from branch to branch; the flowers lilt in the breeze. Inside the gate is truly an enchanted place. It is as though a world once black and white now pulsates with color – everything vivid and alive.

Eagerly we take our key to unlock the gate, but as we move toward the lock, it unlatches itself. It swings wide, inviting us in. Light pours down upon us, and our heart opens. We feel overcome with an indescribable joy. A voice seems to float on the wind, whispering: 'This is the gate of the heart, where gratefulness, love, and kindness flow in and out. This is the gate that mystics, yogis, and other holy ones speak about – the opening of the sacred heart.'

As we stand on the threshold, flower petals drift down around us. On each petal is an image of something we are grateful for – those whom we love, our furred and feathered friends, a good day's work, a healthy body, music and laughter, money to barter for our food – all that blesses our life.

Just inside the gate is a bench, and above it a sign says:

Inside the gate is truly an enchanted place.

SIT HERE
BE
BE GRATEFUL

We lean the quiver against the bench and sit down. Perhaps we can capture our experience in words. As we open our writing tablet to the first page, ready to initiate our **Wand**, we are surprised to discover words printed there:

On this, the first page of your writing tablet, draw or affix images of the blessings of your life – photos, pictures or words from magazines, or other artifacts that signify people, things, and events for which you are grateful. Call this page "That Which Blesses My Life."

__First__ – Consider what blessings you wish to honor here. Turn to the last page of your tablet and make a list of your blessings. List 10 or 20 or more.

__Second__ – Take plenty of time to gather the artifacts or draw the images that you will include on your blessings page. Immerse yourself totally in gathering images and words for what blesses you. The time spent on this task will lay the foundation for the rest of your experience on the Isle of Is.

__Third__ – Affix or draw the images in a way that pleases you. There is no need to hurry. Gratitude knows no time or space. If you wish to use a second or third page, allow your blessings to spill onto additional pages.

__Most importantly__ – Allow yourself to feel grateful for each blessing as you list, gather, and affix images to the page. By thinking and feeling, we experience not just doing gratefulness – writing, drawing, affixing – but __being__ grateful, which is centered in the heart.

Once you have finished your blessings page, you will enter the __Well__, where you will encounter Silence of Mind. Read these directions before entering the Well:

Begin by closing your eyes, breathing, and relaxing into your body. Breathe, relax, and be grateful. Hold in your heart the feeling of gratitude for all your blessings. If your mind drifts to other topics, gently bring it back to all that you are grateful for. You may open your eyes briefly to see again the images and words you have placed in your tablet. Then close your eyes again.

If additional ideas of people, experiences, or things for which you are grateful come to you, know that they come when we are in a state of aware gratefulness. The more we are grateful, the more we recognize to be grateful for. After being in the Well, you can add these ideas to your list on the last page of the tablet. Later you may wish to add them to your blessings page.

CD Track 1:

Deepening Gratitude

Now begin:

Breathe.

Relax.

Feel grateful.

Be in silence for 10 minutes.

Opening our eyes, we notice that everything looks softer than before and at the same time more vibrant. We are truly seeing with new eyes. We feel the bench beneath our hips and the earth beneath our feet. We reach out to touch the blossoms that surround us, the petals delicate and soft to the touch.

But, alas, our hand slips and thorns pierce our skin! We move quickly to pull away and are pricked yet again. With each piercing we are reminded of people, places, and things we find difficult to embrace here in the Garden of Gratitude. Indeed, one thing reminds us of another, and another.

We pick up our **Wand**, and a question comes to mind . . . *For which things am I **not** grateful?*

On the next page of your tablet, write down the things you find difficult to be grateful for. Be as thorough as you can. Call this page "That for Which I Am Not Yet Grateful," being open to the possibility that these too may find their way into your grateful heart. These may be the circumstances of

your personal life, the life situations of others you love, individual people or groups of people, or the problems of the world. Do not concern yourself about the length of the list: it may be very long or very short. What is most important is the honesty of your investigation. Take several minutes to make this list.

The list may not be comfortable to make. Our frustration at not being paid more for our labors. Our recent bout with pneumonia. The merchants who sometimes take advantage of us by raising prices. Our partner's smoking. The commute to work. Gas fumes on the highway. The rooster that wakes us up before dawn. The political system that denies health care to older people.

As we write this list, we see that there are indeed things for which we are not grateful. Often these are places of loss or where our ego was bruised. Loss happens in the realm of time and space, so we think it has a beginning or an end. We may doubt whether we wish to find aspects of these things for which to be grateful. But we decide to be honest with ourselves, taking a few more minutes to add to the list.

A Sleeping Dragon's Tail

A flower near our hand – a gardenia with frilly petals like goose feathers – beckons us to smell. Leaning toward the flower, we think, 'What would happen if we were grateful for the things on this list?'

'Pssst!'

We look around, but there is no one nearby. We lean down again to enjoy the fragrance.

'Pssst! I'm trying to answer your question. I can hear what you're thinking.'

The voice seems to come from the flower. We draw back and look into its center.

'Are you speaking to me?' we ask in disbelief.

The flower nods its head. 'Is this the first time you've heard a flower speak?'

'Yes!' We feel a bit dazed.

'Ah, you'll get used to this here.' The flower lifts its face toward us. 'Flowers have thoughts and feelings, too.'

'We've heard that plants have feelings, but not that they could talk!'

'If you stop and listen, you might hear all kinds of things. There are many wondrous experiences on the island. If you keep your heart and mind open, you will come to know many new things.' The flower's voice is sweet and kind. She nods toward our tablet. 'It was a good thought you had, about the things on your list.'

'About being grateful for the difficult things?'

'Yes. Being grateful for what you consider your blessings is just the beginning. If you notice where it is difficult to be grateful, important things will be revealed to you. Look for places where you are not able to feel grateful. Then see what lessons you might learn from them.'

We look at our list. 'How can we be grateful for *these?*'

'I will show you a story, to help you understand.'

An image begins to form in the center of the flower. It seems impossible, and yet the image moves as we watch, and a story begins to play, a story of another time and place:

A woman named Valerie lives in a blue cottage on a busy street in a small town. Cars and trucks pass Valerie's cottage throughout the day, going to market and back.

In the rainy season the street floods, making it difficult for vehicles to pass, so workmen now come on weekdays to construct a drain for the street. At the end of each day, they leave a tractor parked in Valerie's front yard. Eight feet high and neon orange, it is hard to ignore. Its arm, with an enormous scoop, arches over her driveway, and under it Valerie can drive her car in and out. The scoop itself rests in her front yard, like a napping giant. The tractor is not inconvenient or particularly ugly, but Valerie, like most of us, prefers to gaze at green trees and grass.

For the first few days Valerie doesn't mind. But after two weeks the tractor is still in Valerie's yard, and she wonders when the workers will remove it. After two months, she is tired of looking at it and would like to have it gone. She stares at what has become an irritation, wishing it didn't annoy her.

Valerie, who wants to deepen herself spiritually, considers the possibility of being grateful for the tractor. Perhaps if she can do this, she will be able to let go of her growing irritation. Is there an aspect of this situation that she can be grateful for?

The thought occurs to her that she can be grateful that in the future the tractor will be gone. It seems silly, being grateful for what hasn't happened yet. But why not? She is grateful that her daughter will come for Christmas. Why not be grateful that, at some unknown date, the men will finish their work and remove the tractor from her yard? This thought allows Valerie to be at peace with the present circumstance because she understands that it will change. She can be grateful that change is the nature of life, that nothing ever stays the same.

Finding a reason to be grateful gives Valerie the opportunity to learn a lesson about gratitude. The tractor is no longer an annoyance, but her teacher and friend. Its arch is the arch of gratitude.

We glance up at the wooden arch, thinking about being grateful for change. Certainly, when we are in pain or discomfort, being grateful that change is the nature of life would be helpful – just knowing that the discomfort won't last forever.

'What do you learn from the story?' the flower asks.

'We hadn't considered being grateful for something that hasn't happened yet, or being grateful for change. And we like that Valerie took the time to examine what was irritating her. We would like to do that, too, to learn from difficult situations, so that we can get beyond them.'

'That is good, dear one,' says the flower, nodding. 'This intention will bless your life. It is by entering difficult situations and being present with them that you can grow. Valerie, who wished to grow spiritually from her life's experiences, did well in this situation, for her new perspective is similar to how such an event might be viewed through the eyes of Spirit or God.'

'Because God is grateful for everything?' we ask.

'Yes, God flows graciousness toward every single thing.'

'That's a tall order for us humans – seeing the world as God does.'

'It may seem so now, but why not flow love toward everything? God's love is unconditional, and loving unconditionally is the highest spiritual calling.'

Why not flow love toward everything?

'I never thought of it that way before, that loving unconditionally and being grateful for everything are connected.'

'Indeed, they are the same thing,' says the flower. 'But perhaps I can assist you. Will you pick one item from your list of things you are not yet grateful for? I would be honored to help you with that.'

'Yes, thank you! We would like that.' We examine our list and choose an item: Our sister Jane has borrowed our guitar and not returned it.

'I invite you to visit the Well,' says the flower.

Choose one item from your list – something you haven't thought to be grateful for. Then go to the **Well** *and be in silence for 10 minutes. Here you are in contact with your deepest knowing. Close your eyes and relax into your body. Notice your breath coming in and going out. Notice the sensations of the breath, from your nostrils all the way down to your abdomen. If thoughts come, release them gently and simply notice your breath again.*

At the end of 10 minutes, ask yourself, 'What in this situation can I be grateful for?' When an answer comes, pick up your **Wand** *and write it down.*

If an answer does not come right away, sit quietly and ask again. Allow an answer to come to you, and write it down, even if the answer seems foolish or impossible. Look at your answer and be present with it. Do not judge the answer or decide it is the wrong answer. Simply allow the answer to be the answer.

If there is still no answer, do not judge yourself for this. Simply write in your tablet, 'I am grateful for this situation because I know that there is good in everything.' Even if you do not believe it yet, trust that it is true.

'And what did you discover just now?' asks the flower.

'We saw that we can be grateful that Jane has found a new interest – learning how to play the guitar, something to bring increased joy to her stressful life.' We smile at a new thought. 'And maybe we can get another guitar and play together.'

'Excellent!' says the flower. 'By focusing on gratitude, new blessings have already come to you.'

During this time of reflecting on gratitude, make a daily habit of writing down at least five things you are grateful for. Then add one thing you have not felt grateful for before. Look for an aspect of this situation to be grateful for. Then enter the **Well** *to deepen your gratitude.*

CD Track 1:

Deepening Gratitude

Three Gnomes Away from Home

The flower bids us goodbye, waving her fringed petals, and we lean back on the bench once more. We look around at the arch, the pool in the distance, and the life that is present as birds, blossoms, and trees. Feeling grateful, we glance down at the path that has led us here. Small insects are moving in a line toward a large mushroom, where they form a circle. We peer closer and see that in the center of their circle, in the shade of the mushroom, lies a bird. A dead bird.

A shiver passes through us. What is a dead bird doing on the Isle of Is? Isn't this the place of spiritual upliftment? How can we be grateful for a dead bird? We don't want to think about death – and here it is.

Yet we suspect there is something we can be grateful for in this situation. Why else would it show up in the Garden of Gratitude?

We glance again at the bird and the mushroom that shades its collapsed body. A dew drop forms in the center of the mushroom, creating a prism of moisture in the air.

New thoughts about gratitude come to us, and we have a knowing, from a place beyond our intellect, that the thoughts are being communicated to us by the mushroom. 'The more you use the spiritual tool of gratitude,' it says, 'the easier it is to open the gate of the heart and keep it open. This is especially true when you stretch yourself by seeking the good in experiences you consider difficult or painful. For many, it is difficult to be grateful for challenging or uncomfortable experiences. Cosmic debris inside you, such as feelings of grief or anger, shows you where to look. You can ask yourself, *What is it that prevents me from being grateful for that?'*

In the prism of moisture suspended over the mushroom, another story unfolds from a different time and place. This is the story of Jenny.

Jenny is driving to visit her friend Tina, who is bedridden. Jenny has baked bread and gathered vegetables from her garden to bring to Tina.

She looks forward to seeing her friend, who is good-natured and easy to be around.

Tina's directions to her home involve back routes Jenny has not traveled before. After a while, she seems to be lost. Around her is an industrial section of warehouses and tractor-trailers, gravel piles and chain-link fences. She is driving slowly, studying street signs, when someone in the car behind her honks his horn. *An impatient driver,* Jenny thinks. She glances in the rearview mirror and sees the driver waving frantically. Jenny feels afraid – a strange man wanting her to stop? At the next corner Jenny rolls down her window and leans her head out.

The driver yells out his window. 'Your tire is going flat!' He gestures toward Jenny's left rear tire.

'Thank you!' Jenny waves back and pulls over to let him pass, then gets out to look. Sure enough, the tire is nearly out of air.

In the distance the sounds of traffic are audible. Perhaps if she drives toward the traffic, she can get help.

In a few minutes she emerges onto a well-trafficked road, where a small gas station sits on the corner. *Too small to have a mechanic,* Jenny thinks.

Inside Jenny asks about a mechanic, and the woman behind the cash register shakes her head. As Jenny turns to leave, a man in the corner pops his head up. 'I'm not a mechanic, but what do you need?'

Jenny tells him about the flat. 'I can help with that,' he says.

He ambles out the door behind Jenny and changes the tire while she watches. Flustered about the flat tire, she does not think to call Tina for better directions. She thanks the man and gets in the car.

Jenny heads back to the area where she got lost, but still cannot find the road she is looking for. She drives off in one direction, then returns to her starting place. It occurs to her to wonder what is the purpose of this experience – having a flat tire and getting lost.

As she pulls over to study the map that she found in the glove box, Jenny is startled by the blast of a horn. Looking up, she sees a burly man getting out of a sixteen-wheeler truck. He begins to walk toward her car.

Jenny is frightened and is about to lock her door when the man calls out, 'Hey! Looks like you're lost. Can I help?'

By the time he has pointed her in the right direction, Jenny understands that the day is not about getting a flat tire or getting lost. Rather, it is about noticing that three men assisted her. Because of her experiences as a small child, Jenny was fearful of strange men, even those bearing assistance. Yet three men went out of their way to help her to safety and to her destination.

Jenny realizes that she has a choice about what to tell herself and others about the experience. She can enlarge her fear and distrust by lamenting her brush with danger and her terrible luck. Or she can acknowledge with gratitude what she received from the three men, who brought her gifts just when she needed them.

Later she tells the story to Tina, who responds with a glint in her eyes, 'A flat tire is never a good experience.'

Jenny smiles. 'This one was. I had a lot of help.'

The images of Jenny and Tina fade, and our focus comes back to the prism and the mushroom. We think about Jenny, realizing that if she had been in a place of gratitude, she might not have been afraid. And she would have noticed the blessings along the way, including the gas station that appeared just where she needed it.

Notice the blessings along the way.

As we contemplate the story, we hear rustling on the path. Looking up, we see three dwarf-like men in knickers, flannel shirts, and red pointed caps coming from the direction of the pool. They have rosy cheeks and long beards; they grin widely, their eyes beaming. One carries a hoe over his shoulder; another holds a pickax; the third pushes a wheelbarrow. They are headed out the Gate of Gratitude toward the beach. As they pass, the third one winks. 'Ye haven't seen the last of us,' he says.

Startled, we laugh. Three gnomes, indeed. What is this place? Talking flowers and mushrooms – and gnomes!

The bird, the mushroom, and the circle of insects catch our eye once more. What *is* there to be grateful for in this situation? Certainly, the insects appear to be honoring the bird, and the mushroom is providing shelter. And for all we know, the bird may have been ill and is now released from its body.

'I am here,' says the bird, 'and all is well.'

As we have this thought, we become aware of a presence on our shoulder. It is the spirit of the bird. *'I am here,'* it says, *'and all is well. I no longer need a body, and there is no sadness or pain.'*

Oh! We are taken aback and deeply touched. *'Thank you,'* we say silently. *'Bless you for your thoughts and concerns,'* says the bird's spirit, and it flies on.

With such grace surrounding us, perhaps we will come to a deeper understanding of our own lives. People not returning our phone calls, rain that interferes with our plans, misplaced wallets – even car accidents, flat tires, and getting lost. Sometimes we don't think to look beyond what seems difficult to what is a gift in the experience.

During your daily gratitude practice, ask yourself, 'What in my day, if anything, has seemed difficult? How might I reframe it so that I can express gratitude for this experience?' This practice will point you toward remembering your own Divine nature – an idea that awaits your exploration in further adventures on the Isle of Is.

The Golden Guardians

We are beginning to understand that we can cultivate the ability to find things to be grateful for, regardless of what comes. But how far can we take this? What about the most painful situations? The death of a bird is one thing, but what about the deaths and traumas in our own life?

We stand up and stretch our arms overhead, opening our body and energy to what is next. Perhaps walking around will clear the cobwebs out of our head.

Immediately we catch sight of a silvery web in a nearby tree, as though Nature heard our thoughts. The web begins to vibrate, and we walk closer to look. A spider with a bulbous yellow body and long black legs is smiling at us. We laugh in disbelief. She begins to weave, spelling out the words *The Golden Guardians,* and a story begins to unfold.

The magic of the Garden of Gratitude is bringing us into yet another story. We realize that this is what the garden is about – making things visible so that we can understand.

It is a holiday weekend, and Matt's neighborhood is quiet. In the evening, after celebrating with his family, Matt discovers Sandy, one of his neighbor's golden retrievers, sitting on his veranda.

Matt leads Sandy back to the Greens' house, two doors away, where everything is dark. The backyard gate is broken, and the Greens' second retriever, Chelsea, whines, wishing to be let out. Matt tries to pry open the gate but is unsuccessful, so he chains Sandy to the Greens' front door. Jim and Ellen Green have a toddler, and Matt feels certain they will be home before bedtime.

The next morning Chelsea has joined Sandy on the Greens' front step, having nudged her way out of the gate. The Greens are still not home, and Matt thinks it likely that Jim's dad will come to feed the dogs soon. Certain that Jim would not wish his dogs to be loose, Matt chains them to an ornamental lamppost by the front walk, where they can rest in the shade of a tree.

Matt then drives with his children to the grocery store. When they return, they see both dogs stretched out in the shade. As they drive by, Matt's daughter exclaims, 'Hey, they look like they're dead!'

This seems absurd, but Matt parks the car, and the three of them run back to the Greens' house.

Indeed, the dogs are unconscious. In a panic Matt pumps their chests, lifts their heads and drops them to the ground, even awkwardly tries mouth-to-mouth resuscitation, but the dogs do not revive. With difficulty they load the dogs into the trunk and back seat of his car and drive to the local veterinarian.

After a brief examination, the vet confirms Matt's fear: The golden retrievers are both dead. Neither she nor Matt has a clue as to what killed them. He watches, horror-stricken, as the vet's assistant carries the dogs away.

Matt is mortified at his unintended role in the dogs' deaths and wonders what Jim will do. Matt can never replace Jim's beloved dogs – his faithful guardians – or bring them back to life. He tapes a note on the Greens' door, asking whoever arrives to call him. Half an hour later, Jim's dad drives up, and Matt walks down to see him.

In the Greens' dimly lit living room, Matt describes the events of the last 12 hours. Mr Green is quiet for a few moments before he speaks. 'Sometimes things happen for the best,' he says solemnly. 'Ever since the baby was born, Jim and Ellen haven't known what to do with those dogs.'

Matt is taken aback by Mr Green's ability to accept the dogs' deaths and amazed at his willingness to forgive Matt's role in the tragedy.

Three hours later, after a phone call from Jim's dad, the Greens return from their weekend at the beach. They have figured it out: An electrical short in the lamppost traveled through the metal chain and chokers to electrocute both dogs. They had known about the short circuit, but hadn't bothered to fix it.

'I thought about you all the way home,' Ellen says to Matt. 'What you must be going through. You must feel terrible.'

'We just kept thinking, what if the baby had touched the lamppost?' Jim says.

Matt is deeply relieved, but still distraught about the horrible result. Rather than focusing on their loss or blaming Matt, Ellen and Jim are grateful that the dogs' deaths may have saved their baby's life. The next day Jim and his father dig a three-foot-wide trench across the front yard in order to find the short in the buried wiring.

Matt wrestles with this incident for a long time, feeling guilty for his role and wondering what he should have done differently. Is there a lesson here for him? Should he pull back from helping those who appear to be in need?

Later he comes to understand that it is quite a different lesson. It is about accepting Jim and Ellen's willingness to forgive him, and being grateful for their kindness. Matt, Ellen, and Jim are all able to find gratitude in the midst of tragedy.

The images before us dissolve and once again we find ourselves in the Garden of Gratitude. Nearby, the spider is resting in the web she has woven. We sit quietly, stunned by the story of the golden guardians. It is a story of intense feelings – grief, remorse, and gratitude.

We wonder what in our life feels impossible to be grateful for. We think of the lives of our friends and loved ones, for whom the toughest things have been the death of a sibling, watching their children get involved with drugs, and living with chronic pain. Yet we have seen that the death of a loved one can open up new understandings and a greater connection to Spirit – sometimes even new life directions. A child's difficult journey often forces parents into an examination of their own lives. And constant pain can motivate a deeper relationship to our Higher Power, or a commitment to learn about approaches to alternative healing, which ultimately can assist ourselves and others. For these things, we might become deeply grateful. Through all these experiences, God and Nature have supported others, offering a helping hand.

The spider has been watching us, allowing us time to reflect. 'Why don't you write about your own life?' she says, gesturing toward our Wand and tablet. 'Can you think of something in your life that you can't imagine being grateful for?'

Our father's death immediately comes to mind. He was just 42 when he died, and his death came as a shock. We take out our Wand and gaze into the garden.

*What is one thing in your life that you can't imagine being grateful for? With your **Wand**, write this in your writing tablet.*

*Now close your eyes and be in the silence of the **Well** for 10 minutes. At the end of 10 minutes, ask yourself what there is in this experience to be grateful for. Continue in silence. When an answer comes, ask yourself, 'What else in this experience can I be grateful for?' Write these answers in your writing tablet.*

Allow yourself to fully acknowledge the good that was present in this difficult experience. If you cannot think of any aspect for which you can feel gratitude, allow yourself to be open to seeing what that might be. Allow God, Spirit, or Nature to show you what you have not yet been able to see.

The spider has been busily spinning as we write. When we look up, she glides toward us on a silvery strand. Now she wears a quiver like ours. 'Writing is very beneficial,' she says. 'I have eight hands, and I write all the time. We teach our young ones to write. Part of the weaving of the web is the telling of our story.'

In her web she has written new words: *Free Writing*.

She sees us looking at the web. 'Oh, that.' She giggles. 'That's my note pad – helps me remember what I want to say to island travelers. Sometimes free writing can help you find what is inside you. It takes the focus off your thinking, which can get stuck in a rut, and allows feelings and thoughts to flow freely.'

'We've heard of this,' we say, 'but never tried it.'

The spider dons schoolmarm glasses. 'Begin at the top of a page of paper, allowing whatever is in your mind, heart, body, or emotions to flow onto the page. Do not edit as you write, or stop to think. Write in a free flow – no worries about grammar, punctuation, or anyone seeing what you write.'

She pulls a piece of paper from her quiver and tosses it into our lap. 'Here is an example of free writing that a former traveler wrote. It will show you how writing freely can help you arrive at your true thoughts and feelings.'

We unroll the paper, which is handwritten in dark blue ink.

Okay, so I'm going to free write. About what? Well, my mother has uterine cancer. My task is to write about what I can be grateful for in this? Grateful? You must be kidding. This makes me want to get away from The Isle of Is and forget the whole thing. Why would I want to be grateful for that? What possible good can come of this? Okay, so I'll try. Mum's in pain, and Dad is miserable, terribly afraid that he will lose her. And what about Joe? Well, that's something, isn't it? For the first time that I can remember, he has called Dad and talked to him. How long has it been? 15 years? . . .

Is there anything else I can be grateful for?

'If this were your writing,' says the spider, 'you would not stop here, even though you have found something in the situation to be grateful for. You would explore this aspect of the situation. Then you would ask the question again, to see if there is anything else you can be grateful for.'

'So it is helpful to continue writing beyond one's initial thoughts.'

'Yes, it's very important to keep writing – not to stop when your mind tells you to stop. Would you like to try it?'

We take up our Wand, ready for her next instruction.

*'What in this difficult situation can I be grateful for?' With your **Wand**, write continuously until you fill at least two pages. Write whatever comes to your mind or heart. Do not stop to think. Allow your thoughts and feelings to flow. Your mind may tell you to stop after two sentences, but go further. Write until you find what you can be grateful for – then explore that. Then ask the question again, to see what other aspects of the situation you can be grateful for.*

If an answer does not come in two or three pages, do not concern yourself. Usually this means that you have feelings that must be expressed first – grief or fear or anger. Allow the fullest expression of these feelings that you possibly can. Free-write for two or three pages each day, until you have expressed all you need to express about the situation. At the end of each writing session, ask yourself the question, 'What can I be grateful for in this situation?' and see what comes.

The writing has been very helpful to us. We are surprised to discover that there are, indeed, aspects of our father's death that we can be grateful for. We can be grateful that he is out of pain. We can be grateful that we spent two weeks with him before his death, camping and fishing, while he shared with us something he loved very much. Doing the writing has softened our feelings about his death. Yet we know there is more to express. We will do this again as soon as we can.

The Wizard's Workshop

We are grateful for the assistance we have received from the gardenia, mushroom, and spider, and the stories we've been shown: Valerie's irritation over the tractor parked in her yard; Jenny's fears that were brought up by being lost and having a flat tire in an unfamiliar neighborhood; Matt's grief, guilt, and dismay over being an instrument of killing Jim's dogs. We notice that it was painful feelings that kept each of them from feeling grateful, and once they shifted to a place of gratitude, the painful feelings began to dissipate.

We have begun to understand what gratitude is about and feel ready to move on to other aspects of the Isle of Is. The keys are starting to vibrate. But as we begin to pack our few things into the quiver, we sense that the gardenia and the other beings wish our attention.

'By being grateful, you will become more grateful,' says the white flower. 'By expressing gratitude and behaving in grateful ways, you enter a state of gratitude, a way to be in the world. This is the greatest gift awaiting you on the other side of the gate – a way of being that is joyful and appreciative.'

'And when there is something you can't seem to be grateful about, you can take a closer look,' says the mushroom, shimmering inside prisms of color. 'You can ask yourself what the situation brings up in you that prevents you from being grateful. If you can't find gratitude in a situation, then there is something you aren't yet able to see – a truth you are not yet able to acknowledge. If you wish to know this truth, you can go to the Well or the Wand and ask to be shown.'

Change takes place in the constant present.

The spider nods her tiny head, eyes sparkling. 'But until gratitude infuses your being, it is good to recognize and honor where you are – it is the only place you can work from. You are only in the present; you cannot place your efforts in the past or future. Change takes place in the constant present, and that requires accepting and honoring where you are right now, in this moment.

'If something from your past reaches out to you, it is still with you in the present. You have carried it over from the past. By finding a way to be grateful for it and to acknowledge it in the present, you transform the past event – and those persons who experienced the event with you. This is true even if you do not communicate in the physical realm. It has a new reality. You have rewritten the script.'

Rewriting the script . . . It's a new idea to us, that by being grateful for past situations we can rewrite the script. We wonder if Jane has already returned our guitar. And if our father has received the blessing of our softened feelings.

'Thank you, all of you,' we say, looking from one to the other. 'We are so fortunate to have met you. This place is truly magical – a wizard's workshop – and we are blessed to experience the magic firsthand.'

The spider moves her leg on the web as though she is playing a harp, making sweet tinkling sounds. A dew drop forms as she plays. 'We have covered a lot of web,' she says, smiling. 'Here. Take the essence of these thoughts with you.' She retrieves the dew drop and throws it onto a page in our tablet, where it transforms into words that create a lasting message:

- *Discover gratitude in all things. Be grateful for what you know, think, and feel – all aspects of expression. Be grateful for the smooth path, and for the boulders you must crawl over.*
- *Allow hidden blessings to come to your attention by asking to be shown these blessings. Everything becomes something to be grateful for – whether it has an obvious meaning in the present, or the meaning shows up in some future present.*
- *When you can flow unconditional love toward everything, you will move beyond the realm of judging things as positive or negative, and become willing to live with it as it is – to live in a space of Is-ness. Once you live in the place of Divine gratitude, if you pick up a rose, the thorns will move out of the way of your fingers.*
- *Opportunities to be grateful are everywhere. Be grateful that this is so.*

We close the tablet and tuck it into the quiver. As we wave goodbye to our teachers in the Garden of Gratitude, we think of our friend Anna, who led us here.

'Thank you, Anna,' we say, and we think that she gets the message.

3 | *The Pool of (Ac)knowledge*

The water has taught me to listen;
ye will learn from it, too.
> The Ferryman, *Siddhartha*

In the distance, the pool beckons. Is it our next stop?

We take out the ring of keys. Yes, there is a key with a pool on it. The key begins to pulse with a turquoise glow.

We unfold the map and hold it to the sun. Sure enough, the sun etches a trail a short distance from the Gate of Gratitude to a pool of water. Then words appear: Pool of (Ac)Knowledge. Curious name: Pool of Knowledge? Pool of Acknowledge?

As we start down the trail, musk parrots high in the canopy of trees accompany us, flitting from branch to branch. 'Hello!' we call to the parrots, and they answer, 'Hello!' 'Follow, follow, follow,' they seem to be saying, and we are uncertain who is leading and who is following.

It is a short walk to the pool. Sunlight filters through the branches and shafts of light enter the water, creating a sense of depth even as we approach.

We lean the quiver against the low wall of rocks that rims the pool and gaze about. It appears that we are still in the Garden of Gratitude because the same trees, birds, and flowers are here – rain trees, lorikeets and kingfishers, hibiscus, morning glory, bougainvillea. The pool is clear and jewel-like, the color of an aquamarine. Sitting on the wall, we dip a hand into the water. The light catches just so, and the droplets sparkle between our fingers. We scoop a handful of water and take it to our mouth. It is cool and refreshing.

Our eyes are drawn to an indentation in the rock beside us. Leaning closer, we see it is an impression of a key, carved like the key on the ring. We take out the key again. Indeed, it is identical, and it fits perfectly. As the key slips into place, a light begins to shine from beneath the water, and an image forms – an image of the ferryman standing on the deck of the boat E. Satva.

We are most happy to see him, grateful that we are not alone on this journey.

He tips his captain's hat. 'Greetings, dear traveler. We trust ye are enjoying your visit.'

'Yes, yes, very much.'

The ferryman smiles. 'Ye are doing well, indeed. Ye have made it to the next magnificent place on the Isle of Is.'

We nod. 'It is beautiful here.'

'Ye have arrived at the Pool of (Ac)Knowledge, where ye shall have the opportunity to perceive, acknowledge, and honor all the ways that God and the Universe support ye. This is an important aspect of being grateful, one that magnifies your awareness of the Divine in all things.'

He spreads his arms wide as though to encompass the pool and all its surroundings. 'Many people before your time have known this.' His image recedes and another image forms.

What appears in the pool is a large lake, high in the Andes – Lake Titicaca, on the border between Bolivia and Peru. As we watch, a shaman dressed in serape and wool pants wades into the lake up to his knees. He lifts his arms, much as the ferryman just did, and calls on Great Spirit, expressing gratitude for Spirit flowing through him to bring healing to others. He looks like an ordinary man, yet there is a light about him, and he is remarkable for his wisdom and presence. On his face is a beatific smile.

This image fades, and another appears of Hopi elders dancing around a blazing fire. They chant and raise their arms to the night sky – an infinite pool of stars. Their chant rings to the heavens as they thank Father Sky for bringing rain for their crops when they need it. As they continue to dance, clouds move in obscuring the stars, and lightning sparks in the distance.

The image dissolves, and yet a third scene appears, this one from ancient Egypt. On the banks of the River Nile, astrologers look into a golden bowl crafted in the shape of the sun. We sense that they gaze into the bowl for the purpose of acknowledging and honoring the sun god Ra. Indeed, they raise their faces to the sky, where the heavenly body, the sun Ra, follows its path over the Earth. The astrologers acknowledge their eternal connection to Ra, who for them symbolizes all-powerful God. The sun overpowers the scene, transforming the pool before us into a bright golden light.

The pool has gone through the colors of lake, night sky, and sun.

As the light dims, the face of the ferryman returns. 'What think ye of these dreams?' he asks.

'We're in awe of the magic that brings these other worlds into view. It's inspiring to see other people honoring their concept of God.'

'Indeed, this is the "acknowledge" aspect of the pool that ye stand before. They are acknowledging the support they receive from Spirit. By expressing gratitude to Spirit, to God, they open the door for even more blessings in their lives. Do ye know, dear one, what a synchronicity is?'

'Yes: a coming together of two events in a way that one may have thought unlikely.'

'And to what purpose? Know ye that?'

'They are two events that seem like a coincidence, but actually they are not by chance.'

'Tis a good answer. But if not by chance, then what?'

For whose purpose?
Spirit's? God's? Ours?

We consider this question. We're not sure how two events might come together on purpose. For whose purpose? Spirit's? God's? Ours?

The ferryman seems to hear our thoughts. 'Exactly. All three. 'Tis the way it is. Events come together because it is what ye have asked for, and because it serves a greater purpose – God's purpose, Spirit's purpose. Indeed, it is how Spirit acknowledges and interacts with ye.

'By acknowledging a synchronicity,' he continues, 'ye become aware of the Divine perfection that is all around ye. Deepening your knowing about synchronicity will open ye to participating more fully in Spirit's Divine play.'

'We think that we perceive synchronicities when they happen,' we say.

'It seems that they happen more frequently at some times than at others.'

'Aye,' says the ferryman. 'For most people, synchronicities happen one moment here, one moment there. But they will increase as ye pick up your Wand and go to the Well, until they seem to come in a stream, one after the other. This process will bring ye closer and closer to knowing that all is Divine perfection, which includes ye and your life. Therefore, understanding synchronicities is important on your present journey, and on all your future present journeys.'

All is Divine perfection, which includes ye and your life.

'Sometimes our life doesn't feel like Divine perfection.' We laugh. 'But then we didn't think we could feel gratitude for our father's death, either.'

'It is good to hear ye laugh.' The ferryman grins. 'Good humor will assist ye on the island.

'And now,' he bows slightly, 'the knowledge of the pool will provide some stories that are chosen just for ye. Three stories tell of the material aspect of our lives. They are about two people and their experience of buying a house. We invite ye to look for the message about synchronicity in each one.'

Message of the Maori Man

We peer into the pool, eager for the first story to play. As we watch, an image forms of a man and woman in a car, from the modern realm we left behind. The man is driving, and the woman is leaning forward, glancing at street signs they pass along the way.

John and Kate are shopping for a house. They intend to create a healing center in the house, where they will teach meditation and connection to Spirit, and where they will also live.

They have investigated several neighborhoods and today are focusing on a neighborhood that is probably out of their price range, but one they feel drawn to explore.

Driving toward the neighborhood, they pass a large-boned man with earth-brown skin who is walking on the side of the road. He is wearing a loose-knit hat and a jogging suit.

John recognizes the man's features as Maori. 'I've visited New Zealand and spent time with Maori healers, but I never thought I'd see a Maori here.'

Kate nods in agreement. Indeed, the man is much larger than most people who live in these parts and he has Polynesian features: golden skin, black hair, a strong jaw, and a broad nose. Around his neck is a piece of carved pounamu, the precious greenstone sacred to Maori.

As their car turns into the neighborhood, they comment on what a curious event it is. John's Maori friends are expected to visit John and Kate within the month, and they puzzle over why a Maori might be here now.

Later, on a different street, going a different direction, they see the man again. 'Amazing.' John shakes his head. 'The same man, twice in the same day.'

They continue to look at houses for another hour. After driving through the area and preparing to head back home, Kate and John see the Maori man yet again, while Kate is driving.

'Stop the car,' John says. But there is no place to pull over, and by the time Kate has turned the car around, they see no sign of him.

Kate and John never see the Maori man again, but John knows that the visitation carries a message meant for the two of them.

As the story fades from view, we understand that we are to take out our writing pad and **Wand**, then answer three questions:

'What is the story about?' Free-write. Let the words flow without trying to figure out the right answer. When an answer comes to you, proceed to the next question. 'Is the appearance of the Maori man a synchronicity? If so, what is its purpose?' Again, free-write until an answer comes. Finally, 'What can we learn about synchronicities from this incident?'

When we have finished writing, the ferryman's image appears in the pool again. 'Do ye think this is a synchronicity?' he asks.

'Yes! The Maori appeared three times – a spiritual number, isn't it? But is it Spirit communicating to John and Kate, or does this particular Maori have a message for them?'

'Ye are right about the synchronicity. And it is a very good question. Since the man is not someone John knows personally, we might conclude that it is Spirit speaking through the Maori. However, even if John knew him, it would be Spirit using the Maori to communicate with him. Spirit will use whatever has meaning for ye, to allow the message to be most clear.' The ferryman pauses. 'What might be Spirit's message? And why speak through a Maori?'

'Because of John and Kate's spiritual connection to the Maori people, perhaps Spirit appeared as a Maori so that they would know that the message was just for them.'

'Aye, very good. And the message?'

'That John and Kate should continue to look in that neighborhood? It's like Spirit is affirming that they are on the right track.'

'Ye have done very well. And the final question: What might be the specific learning here?'

We think for a bit. 'We don't know.'

'The Maori's appearance is miraculous, don't ye think? Supernatural. Seemingly impossible. This story is about acknowledging that Spirit is able to work magic. John and Kate are being called upon to honor the miraculous workings of Divinity. Spirit, Nature, or God will go to any lengths to open the channel of communication.'

'But what if we don't believe in magic?'

'Ye don't need to believe in magic. Just honor the power and majesty of Divine Presence. Spirit can manifest itself in seemingly magical ways.'

Spirit can manifest itself in seemingly magical ways.

We look down at our writing tablet to make notes about honoring the workings of Spirit. As we do, words appear on the page:

*Dear traveler, for one week record with your **Wand** the synchronicities you experience. Do this at the end of each day. You will go first to the **Well**, then close your eyes and express gratitude for all the support you receive. Be in silence for 10 minutes or longer, then take up your **Wand** to write down unexpected happenings, things that have gone smoothly . . . even miracles. All the gifts of synchronicity.*

Take a few moments to do this now. Close your eyes and be in silence for 10 minutes. Then record at least three synchronicities that come to mind – experiences you have had in the last few days. Allow yourself the time to write down everything that comes to mind. It may be five or ten or more synchronicities. Honor all the synchronous events you can remember, for it is in **honoring** *that your awareness increases and the power of Spirit magnifies in your life. Express gratitude for each of the synchronicities.*

Do this for the next six days, examining each day at the close of day. If you regularly meditate on a daily basis, do this as an aspect of your meditation time.

We review the list we have made: running into Anna at the supermarket, where we first learned about the trip to the sacred island; the fact that there was a boat leaving for the island the very next week; the ferryman, whose kindness is assisting us on this incredible journey; finding the map and keys on the beach. Many synchronicities have occurred just since arriving at the Island of Is, as though the entire trip is a synchronicity. God/Spirit has infused our experience with 'Divine Presence' – and we like that term.

Paint It 'Putty'
As we turn back to the pool, a second scene with John and Kate begins to form. They are walking in the neighborhood they had explored earlier.

It is two months later, and Kate and John have found the perfect house in the neighborhood that the presence of the Maori man acknowledged. They are waiting for final approval from the bank to finance the house. The dwelling includes three rooms for their workshops and healing work, and a spacious bedroom upstairs. Meanwhile, the sellers, who are in the process of renovating the house, are ready to paint the exterior.

This day, on a walk in their new neighborhood, Kate sees a color she would like for the exterior trim – an earthy gray color. She points it out to John. 'The color of putty,' she says.

John, formerly in the construction trades, notes that 'not many folks would call it that.'

The next day they meet with their realtor, who has been talking to the sellers about paint colors. 'They've chosen some colors, but if you'd like to choose your own, they will accommodate you,' she says, 'as long as the colors are fairly neutral. They don't want to take a chance that the bank will turn down your application for a loan. Then they'd have to find another buyer, who might not like your color choices.'

'Kate's picked out a color for the trim,' John tells her.

'Well, the sellers were thinking of painting it putty,' the realtor says.

John smiles. 'That's exactly the word Kate used.'

'That's quite a coincidence!' says the realtor.

'Not a coincidence,' John says. 'It's a message of acknowledgement from Spirit – a synchronicity.'

'Oh,' she says, nodding. 'I see. There's more to this house sale than meets the eye.'

Not a coincidence? We know about synchronicities, but this is an odd one, isn't it? A paint color? Why would Spirit speak in paint colors? Especially after John and Kate have already found their house.

Why would Spirit speak in paint colors?

'Do ye think it was a synchronicity?' asks the ferryman, coming freshly into view.

'We think so, but we aren't sure about Spirit's message to John and Kate.'

'Indeed, 'tis a synchronicity. Synchronicities always have the purpose of expressing Spirit's support – and John and Kate certainly recognize Spirit's continuing support for their house purchase – but there is also a particular purpose and a new learning here. Who do ye think is most impressed or inspired by the synchronicity?'

We think for a moment. 'The realtor?'

'Exactly so. This synchronicity is partly for the benefit of the realtor. But there are others as well.' The ferryman pauses, then proceeds, happy to explain. 'The sellers, too, who have chosen the color putty. They will hear the story from the realtor. John and Kate, the realtor, and the sellers – all will be aware of the synchronicity and its purpose. They will realize they played their part, and that Spirit played its part as well. The synchronicity will solidify the sellers' feeling that John and Kate are the right buyers for the house.'

'We hadn't thought about the sellers, but we can see how the synchronicity might be a relief to them. For one thing, they won't have to change the paint color for John and Kate!' Then a new idea comes to us. 'And the realtor and sellers would not have thought about Spirit's role if John had been silent about it. It was necessary for him to comment on it.'

'Aye. If John had not spoken about it, neither the realtor nor the sellers would have received the understanding, would they?'

This insight is a valuable one. Synchronicities are a way for others to understand Spirit's support. And we – each of us – can help in this process by noticing and pointing them out when they happen.

Immersed in the Realm

Excited about the new things we are learning, we turn once more to the pool, where Kate and John are walking through a large hardware store. Such a curious thing, these stories of experiences others are having back home.

Kate and John have just moved their belongings into the new house. But because of the renovation, the windows lack curtains, shades, and blinds.

At the local hardware store, the clerk tells them it will take nine weeks to order blinds and shades and have them installed. Nine weeks is a long time to wait, especially because of their workshops and healing work, but John and Kate decide to proceed, as this store is nearer their new home than others.

John makes an appointment for Mr Lee, the installer, to come to the house and measure the windows. 'It will be about three weeks before he can come,' the clerk tells John.

John grins at the clerk. 'We can allow Spirit to assist us in this happening much sooner.'

The next day Mr Lee telephones John to say that the oddest thing has happened. He was scheduled to come to Willow Road today – which is just three city blocks long – to measure windows at another house, and has just discovered Kate and John's order for their house on Willow Road. Two houses on the same short road. What a coincidence! Would it be okay if he came today?

'Yes, it would,' John agrees.

John hopes the installer will come in the morning, because John is meeting with clients at home in the afternoon, and measuring for blinds would be an interruption. John takes a moment to be silent with the situation and visualizes Mr Lee coming before lunch. He thinks, 'I can allow this to happen in a convenient manner.'

Mr Lee drives up at 11:00 am, and John thanks Spirit silently for the assistance. When he has finished measuring, Mr Lee tells John it will likely be three weeks before the order comes in. John says to Mr Lee that he will allow it to happen sooner than that.

One week later a call from the hardware store confirms that the order has arrived earlier than expected, and would it be alright if Mr Lee comes to install the blinds at his earliest convenience, likely in about three weeks?

John and Kate are not surprised when he shows up four days later to install the blinds.

As the story fades, we wait for the ferryman to appear in the pool, but he does not. Hmmm. We stand up and walk around the area, looking at the trees and flowers. No doubt we are to enter the Well or write with the Wand.

The stories of John and Kate are having an interesting effect. All sorts of events and experiences in our life are coming up for review. As our mind notes each experience, we find ourselves rethinking what occurred – reframing it as a synchronicity. Is it possible that all these experiences were, in fact, synchronicities? If paint colors and appointments for blinds are synchronicities, we can hardly imagine how many small events in our own life are synchronicities as well.

Even small events are synchronicities.

'Ye have discovered something, we see.' It is the ferryman's voice, and we return to the edge of the pool.

'Even small events can be synchronicities,' we say.

'Aye, the smallest events. If ye acknowledge the minute, ordinary, daily events – every time something works easily or smoothly or well – then the number of synchronicities will increase vastly, as will your own awareness of the role of Spirit in your life. Ye will become more and more attuned to Spirit.'

We pick up our writing tablet. 'We wish to write down some of the events in our own life, as a way to help us remember the importance of acknowledging synchronicities.'

Many thoughts come to mind . . . the sale on lamps at the department store just as we were desiring to purchase a lamp . . . the fact that our usually busy friend 'happened' to be free the night we wanted to go to a movie . . . yesterday, when we needed a bandage for a small cut, and there was just one left. We write these down, and more.

> *Record with your **Wand** all the tiniest events and synchronicities that come to mind, as many things as you can think of. Use free writing. "Oh, yes, and then there was the time that …"*
>
> *Now go to the **Well** to be in silence for 10 minutes. Then, with eyes closed, express gratitude to Spirit for all the support you can remember and for all the support you cannot remember.*

When we open our eyes, the ferryman is waiting for us. 'There is one more aspect of the stories about Kate and John for ye to note,' he says. 'What was their purpose in buying the house?'

'To live there.' We think for a moment. 'Oh, and to do healing work.'

He nods. 'Aye, the work of Spirit.'

We wait for more explanation, then realize that the ferryman is allowing us to get the understanding.

'Are there more synchronicities if we do the work of Spirit?' we ask. It seems the obvious question.

'Sometimes people do the work of Spirit but haven't acknowledged it to themselves. More often, they have not placed the work of Spirit in its proper perspective; that is, first in their lives. When they do so – as Kate and John have done – Spirit offers even more support, and the synchronicities – the miracles – abound. Ye see, don't ye, that all those events we label as synchronicities are truly miracles, for they are blessed events.'

'And will we be considering this further at other locations on the Isle of Is?' we ask the ferryman.

'Indeed, ye will.' He winks.

'We have a question for *ye,*' we say, laughing. 'What about all these threes? Three stories. Three sightings of the Maori man. Three sets of people who play a part in the story of putty. Three time periods of anticipated waiting for the blinds – of three weeks each!'

'Divine synchronicities?' he asks.

We laugh again. 'And for what purpose?'

He waits for us to figure it out.

'For us to write it on our list of synchronicities?' we ask.

'And for ye to see how the Universe creates them on your behalf. Three is a holy number found in many ancient religions, indigenous cultures, and modern philosophies: three aspects of God in Christianity; three aspects of Absolute Being in the Vedas; the ego, id, and super ego of modern-day psychiatry; the upper, middle, and lower worlds of shamanism; Polynesia's delineation of the three selves. When three shows up in your life, ye might take notice.'

Suddenly we realize that the threes have shown up not only for John and Kate's benefit, but also for our own understanding as a traveler on the Island of Is.

The ferryman's image draws closer. 'One last knowing awaits ye here, however.'

'Is this the "knowledge" part of acknowledge? We've been wondering about that.'

The ferryman smiles. 'Since ye have progressed this far, it means that ye are spiritually ready to look into this pool of your ego self and your spiritual Self. Acknowledging synchronicities is like looking in the mirror to acknowledge one's Presence. The pool is here to acknowledge the truth of what ye are. There is no knowledge greater than this.' The ferryman's image dissipates, but his voice remains. 'Look now in the pool, at your Self.'

We take a deep breath and, clasping the rocks, lean over to view our reflection in the pool. At first what we see is our face – familiar, just as we saw it last. But then the pool begins to glow, as a radiance gradually envelops our being. Within seconds, our face and body and the surrounding area have been transformed into a golden white light.

We are astonished, and our thought is to pull back, but our hands cannot let go of the rocks. We continue to experience and see ourselves as this expanding field of light.

This field of light is your Divine Presence.

'This is your Divine Presence,' the ferryman says. 'Seems too good to be true, does it? It is Truth.'

We are held here, viewing the reflection for a few more seconds before pulling back.

What an incredible experience! How can it be? Feelings and thoughts of doubt flood our mind and body. Is that truly what we are? It can't be. And yet . . . if it is so, then perhaps future Isle of Is experiences will lead us to understand more.

The ferryman's voice begins to fade. 'The answers ye seek are within,' he whispers. Then he is gone at last, and the pool has returned to its aqua color.

We look around, still stunned by the experience. Perhaps it will help if we sit in silence. We close our eyes and breathe deeply, resting in the stillness within.

A few minutes later, a rustle in the bushes causes us to look up. Emerging from the brush are the gnomes in velvet hats and fitted waistcoats, without the tools they carried before. We notice that they walk with their toes pointing inward, in boots made of felt. Delighted, we laugh out loud, and they chuckle in return. They tap their hats in acknowledgement. 'Here's to ye!' says the first gnome.

As they pass, on their way into the brush, we see that their waistcoats are embroidered on the back.

YE – says the first coat.

ARE – says the second.

DIVINE.

4 | *The Briar of Beliefs*

Shut ye eyes in order to see.
        Paul Gauguin

As the gnomes' footsteps fade into the forest – swish, krinkle, krunch – we pick up the key from the indentation in the rock and wonder what will be next.

Doubts begin to pry their way into our mind. Certainly it is beautiful here, and some of our experiences have been quite illuminating. But Divine white light as our reflection? And talking to a ferryman in a pool? If our friends saw us, they'd think we were taking hallucinogens! Divine, indeed! There must be trickery and tomfoolery in the pool.

We lean over to catch our image in the water again, but it is getting late and around us the light is fading. All that appears is the muted reflection of shadowy branches. We begin to worry that we are alone and wonder where we will sleep.

Glancing around, we see no opening in the brush. Even the path that led from the Gate of Gratitude has vanished. The forest has grown thick, closing us in. What are we doing here, anyway? Anna got us into this, and where is she now? Why did we leave everything behind to visit this island?

*The more we fret,
the more tangled grow
the briars around us.*

The more we fret, the more tangled grow the briars around us. We hold up the map, but there's not enough sunlight to etch the next section of trail. We study each key until we find one with an image of a tree and brambles, but it does not glow or vibrate.

Sitting down on the rock wall, we consider our options. 'Ferryman! Anna!' we call silently. But they do not come. What did the ferryman say as he departed? 'The answers ye seek are inside.' That could mean going to the Well or writing with the Wand. Okay, we will try going to the Well. We close our eyes, but moments later open them again; it's not working.

Perhaps we could practice being grateful. We close our eyes again and think, *We are grateful for all the support we have received thus far.* We remember, item by item, our list of synchronicities. Again, this time aloud: 'We are grateful for all the support we have received thus far.'

Then we wonder: If we are grateful only for the past, will it change anything in the present? Perhaps if we are grateful for the support we are receiving now, that will allow more support to show up. We decide to change the words: 'We are grateful for all the support *we receive.'* Breathing deeply, we begin to relax. We sit silently for several minutes.

In the silence, the idea comes to point the bramble key at the forest surrounding us. Slowly we open our eyes, then stand up and begin to turn in a circle. When we are about three-quarters of the way around, the brush rustles, and we stop. The briars begin to part, making an opening large enough to walk through. Suddenly the key starts to vibrate and pulse with a deep green light. Thank goodness! With a sigh of relief, we sling the quiver over a shoulder and step through the opening. Perhaps we gain something by going into silence, after all.

Inside, there is only more brush. The branches reach toward us with their thorns, catching at us with sharply pointed fingers. *How did we get here?* we moan inwardly. *And why are we here?* A briar grabs our shirt. We try to pull away, but the more we struggle, the tighter its grip. The more we fear being in the briar, the greater becomes the fear.

A wind sweeps through the brush, its voice a whisper: 'Be still. Be calm. Cease doing and be aware of me: I am the ever-present breath of Nature; let my breeze become your breath. When you can be still and aware, calmness will prevail.'

Be calm. Be still. We stop struggling, and, indeed, the briar fingers loosen their grip. We become more aware of the space around us.

The opening has closed behind us, and we try not to be frightened. Be still. Breathe deeply. Briars surround us completely, creating a chamber 10 or 12 feet across – twice the distance from fingertip to fingertip. Sunlight pierces the branches to our right, forming an ellipse in the center of the chamber. We spread our map in this light, and as we do, the sun etches a trail from the pool to a thicket. Words appear, scribed by an invisible artist: *The Briar of Beliefs*.

What beliefs? And what are we to do here? Briars twist this way and that, allowing no way out. We look around and notice an old tree held in the briars' clutch.

Moving closer to study the tree, we feel compassion for its plight and reach through the briars to touch its trunk. The prickly branches slowly withdraw, revealing letters carved in an ancient script. Failed growth falls away, exposing the words

Divinity Is Your True Identity

Glimmers of Reality

We read the statement aloud, our voice reverberating through the chamber. Then we hear an ancient, resonant voice added to ours, and we look up.

'It is I, Sentinel of the Briar,' says the tree. 'It's an interesting synchronicity, is it not, that you find yourself in the Briar of Beliefs, where travelers such as yourself come to discover what keeps them from believing they are Divine? 'Tis your doubts and fears that have brought you here.'

'What do you mean? Divinity is a matter of belief?' We are astonished.

'Indeed,' says the tree, bowing its upper branches. 'One can believe many things about Divinity and one's own true nature. What is it that you believe?'

'It's quite a stretch to believe we're Divine, that's for sure. No one ever told us that is what we are.'

The tree leans toward us as though to share a secret. 'You are absolutely right. Your parents, churches, and society have not told you – few of these know who you really are. Many were never exposed to the truth themselves.

And if they do know about your Divinity, they may be unwilling to share that knowledge with you. Some churches, for example, feel that people aren't ready to know this. It is a way for them to keep their followers coming back. They fear that if everyone knew they were Divine, there would be no need for the church.'

'But how can we believe it if others around us don't?'

'Well, perhaps you can't.' The tree tosses its branches. 'But then again . . . perhaps you can. You see, most of humanity is caught in their briar of beliefs, and only a few make it to this island.'

'We have many beliefs, of course, but we weren't aware that they formed a briar.'

Most of humanity is caught in their briar of beliefs.

'The briar is an accumulation of restrictive beliefs,' says the tree. 'One limiting belief links to another, and soon they begin to pull us away from our true self. The morning glory is a beautiful plant, but a mass of its tangled vines wrapped around a tree will eventually overpower the tree and pull it down.

'Humans can be stuck in a place of misunderstanding, a place of not knowing, because of their briar. They are so caught up in what they think they need for survival that they do not question their beliefs. Yet Divine teachers such as Jesus remind us that even the lilies of the field are taken care of. Why wouldn't we be taken care of, too?' The tree's voice becomes hushed. 'By the way, parables like this were Jesus's way of helping people approach the truth that they are Divine.'

Jesus thought we were Divine? We consider this idea. 'Some of us humans don't believe that we'll be taken care of – *this* human, for example!' We point to our own heart.

'Many humans hold onto certain beliefs regardless of how those beliefs limit them. Then the beliefs become like a prison.' The tree crosses its smallest branches in front of its face, imitating prison bars. 'It's important to look at your beliefs to see how they have limited you.'

'It's hard to describe what we really believe, or to know which beliefs may be limiting us.'

'Ah, well, that is where I can help. Why don't you sit here, on my root?' The tree points to a large, smooth root at its base. 'Sit, and I will tell you some common beliefs that prevent people from knowing they are Divine.'

As we sit down, the root curves around, forming a seat. We lean back and look up at the tree.

'Here – for your consideration.' The tree drops a scroll, which drifts into our lap and unfurls to reveal a list of beliefs about Divinity and being Divine.

A List of Beliefs

1. *I don't really believe in God or Spirit, so Divinity is troubling to me, at best. I don't think it exists.*

2. *I don't know whether God or Spirit exists, but I doubt it, so Divinity is irrelevant to me.*

3. *I don't believe that Divinity is my true identity. God is Divine; humans are not.*

4. *I believe that a few select others are Divine – Buddha, Jesus, the Virgin Mary – but not me. They were destined to have a Divine role in humanity. Being Divine is not an option for me.*

5. *I don't believe it is desirable to know myself as Divine; I might feel that I was above other people. Besides, there's work to do in the world. How will it get done if I sit around meditating all the time?*

6. *I don't know whether I believe I am Divine or not. It's all new to me. I'd like to know more about it.*

7. *I've had glimmers of the reality of my Divinity and wish to learn how I might experience it more consistently.*

'The first two beliefs – or non-beliefs – are shared by as much as one-third of humanity,' says the tree. 'The non-believer and the agnostic, as they might label themselves, to their credit do not bow down to a Divine being who hangs out on a cloud, nor do they fear a God who sits in judgment of what they do. But they do miss out on the reality that everything is permeated with an interactive, Divine intelligence.'

'So what are their chances of coming to know Divinity?' we ask.

'The Divine realm operates for the raising of consciousness of all souls,' says the tree. 'It is not vested in the level of belief or disbelief, but flows grace to all beings evenly, equally, beyond the realm of judgment. Many non-believers and agnostics operate from a high moral ground, yet they are unaware that there is more for them to see. It would be like a scientist looking into a powerful microscope and seeing an organism for the first time – discovering the existence of something they were not previously aware of. Myriad possibilities would open to them, thus shattering their former beliefs.'

'It would be like seeing Divinity for the first time?' we ask.

'Divinity can unfold itself in many ways, and it takes just one moment to shatter a belief and open a new door.'

It takes just a moment to shatter a belief and open a new door.

The tree points to the list. 'The third belief – that God is Divine but humans are not – allows at least for the existence of Divinity. But if humans are not Divine, then how can one recognize and honor the existence of the individual soul, which is a basic teaching of many religions? The belief also eliminates the possibility of Divinity being the nature of all things.'

'The belief that "God is Divine but humans are not" is a common teaching of Christianity, Judaism, and Islam, isn't it?'

'Yes,' says the tree. 'Most modern religions have removed themselves from their original, inspired teachings. Many Christian churches, for example, teach a separation between humans and God, even though Jesus said that the kingdom of God is within. Isn't Divinity the essence of the kingdom of God? Other religions – Hinduism, Buddhism, Sufism – as well as many indigenous peoples recognize that Divinity pervades everything, including humans.'

We wonder what it would be like to believe that Divinity pervades everything.

'The fourth belief, that a few select others are Divine, is similar to the second,' the tree continues. 'Here, God or Spirit has infused certain human beings with Divine qualities. The particular list doesn't matter – the Pope, Mohammed, Abraham, Mother Teresa, priests, rabbis, gurus, Sunday School teachers – you get the idea. These individuals are supposedly better than others, more blessed, or closer to God.'

'We were taught that even if you work very hard, you may earn a place in Heaven, but you can't earn Divinity.'

'Yes, you were told that you were born imperfect, that you are a sinner. But is a rose imperfect? Is a hummingbird imperfect?' The tree has a kind expression on its rough bark face.

'We don't think so. Flowers and birds were created perfect. Even crushed flowers are perfect in their own way. So is it our beliefs that distort our vision, keeping us from seeing perfection?'

'Exactly,' the tree says. 'Have you seen how certain beliefs create imperfection in your own life?'

Our thoughts turn to Luke, a warm-hearted, thoughtful friend whose parents believed that he was born full of sin, and it was their job to help him become what God wanted him to be – a docile, quiet child. Luke's church and family punished him when he was a curious and energetic child, intent on exploring the world. We remember the song, "Red and yellow, black and white, they are precious in his sight . . . ." Wouldn't these precious children be perfect in God's sight? And wouldn't that include Luke?

Now, as an adult, Luke is struggling to feel that he is good, not marred by birth or by those early abuses.

The tree knows our thoughts. 'Your friend illustrates just one instance of someone who has been indoctrinated into limiting beliefs. The essential nature of all children – indeed, of all humans – is Divinity. With more self-confidence,' says the tree, 'Luke could instill a greater spiritual presence in his children and pass on his experience of Divinity to them.'

The essential nature of all humans is Divinity.

'Oh, yes; we see.' We make a mental note to let Luke know that we think he is generous and kind.

The tree continues, 'Some people believe that it's not desirable to know oneself as Divine, for various reasons. They fear that their ego will become inflated – like Narcissus, enraptured with his reflection in the water, or in modern terms, they will develop a superiority complex, feeling themselves better than everyone else. Another fear is that they will lose touch with the needs of the world. In reality, both of these fears are groundless.'

'We look forward to hearing more about that belief! It is definitely one of our own beliefs about Divinity.'

'Some people, like yourself, come to the Isle of Is with an open mind, as in Belief #6. They have not previously entertained the possibility that they are Divine, but they are willing to consider that it's true.'

'We do feel open-minded about it. And curious about whether we'll actually believe that we're Divine by the time we leave the island.'

'Ah! We trees have an idea about that!' The tree's leaves seem to blaze in the late afternoon sun, as though shining light on its comments. 'And what about the last belief? Have you had glimmers of your Divinity by now?'

'We have. Thanks to Anna, the ferryman, and the island.'

'This is good. You are on the threshold of understanding your true nature.' The tree points to our quiver. 'And now it's time for you to write. I will relish being in unity with my brothers and sisters' – the tree sways and spreads its limbs as though to embrace the entire forest – 'while you write about where you are in relation to each belief.'

*Take up your **Wand** and write, reflecting on where you are with each of the seven beliefs. If you have other beliefs related to your own Divinity, write these down as well and comment on them. The more fully you explore the beliefs, the more beneficial the writing will be.*

*When you are finished writing, go to the **Well** and be in silence for 10 minutes or more. Say the statement 'Divinity is my true identity' silently in your mind, then be present with the feelings it brings up. Feel the sensations in your body, but make no judgment about what your mind believes. It is what it is.*

Writing takes us deep into ourselves. After we have written and sat in silence, we open our eyes to see the tree regarding us closely. 'I can feel the love in your heart,' it says.

'And we in yours,' we say.

Drop the 'Lief – and Be

'Are you ready to review those beliefs?' the tree asks.

We nod. 'Yes, we're ready.'

'Let's look at #1. People who don't believe in God or Spirit may be reacting to someone else's concept of God, perhaps one that their family or church imposed on them when they were children. Society's view of God or Spirit may not be their particular experience. But if we look at Nature, we see that beauty and order underlie everything, from the micro level to the macro level. What accounts for this order?'

We see that beauty and order underlie everything.

The tree bends to pick up a seed pod. 'If you are an acorn or a seed, you cannot understand the total tree. The state of Divinity goes beyond the mind. You may do your utmost to understand, but the mind finds it unfathomable.'

'So am I a seed?' we ask.

'Yes, you are, dear one, with a fine heart, mind, and spirit. But unlike a seed, you don't have to take 30 years, or 300 years, to become a mature tree. Within you is the potential for understanding and knowing the vastness of Divine creation. Knowing oneself as Divine happens very quickly here on the island.'

This resonates with our heart and our internal understanding. Sometimes we feel a great potential inside us – a sprout ready to burst forth, a bud ready to bloom. 'We do believe in Spirit,' we say, 'and we can clearly see order in Nature.'

'This is a solid foundation for expanding your awareness,' says the tree. 'And what about the person who doesn't know if God or Spirit exists, and for them Divinity is irrelevant?'

'It seems similar to the first, but the person is more open to the possibility that God or Spirit exists. They just don't have proof.'

'Ah, yes, proof.' The tree nods its upper limbs. 'Perhaps they should look at recent scientific evidence that all matter and all space are composed of energy, which actually communicates with itself. Scientists have even found that the energy responds to the one who is observing it, matching the expectations of the observer!'

'We've never heard of such a thing. Can this be true?'

'Indeed, the truth of this is so powerful and evident now, that science can no longer deny it. Our history is full of examples of people not believing something until someone could prove it. At one time, almost everyone believed the world was flat, and no one knew about the existence of bacteria and viruses.'

'So Divinity can now be seen in a microscope?' We smile at the idea.

'Essentially, yes, what *we* mean by Divinity: that vibrational order of the Universe that demonstrates vast intelligence.'

'It seems that agnostics are closer to recognizing Divinity than non-believers.'

The tree smiles kindly. 'Everyone is as close as the present moment, if their beliefs will allow them to see it.'

We hold up the list, and the tree points to #3. 'The third belief is a stumbling block for many. They believe in a supreme Presence. Their minds can understand that this Presence is omnipotent, omniscient, omnipresent, all-seeing. Yet they exclude themselves from it. If this Presence is indeed everywhere, how can it exclude you?'

The tree waits for this idea to soak in. 'For some, Divinity is an *aspect* of who they are. They know they have a mind, a heart, a body, and a spirit or soul. But they identify with the mind or ego part, not the spirit or Divinity part. Identifying with the me-ness – the ego – creates the thought, "I am separate from Divinity. I can have it all around me, even inside me, but it isn't me."'

'That describes what we believe. We know that there is spirit or Divine energy *within* us, but we haven't thought that *was* us.'

'When you die, you will leave your body. You know that, don't you?'

'That's what we've been told.'

'This means you must be the soul or spirit, because you aren't the body, and you aren't *in* the body any more.'

'It makes sense, and we know that's right. But we seem to have this contradictory belief that we can't be Divine!'

'A valuable observation,' says the tree. 'Often humans have contradictory beliefs, but even when they are aware of it, they hang onto the beliefs.'

'Why is that?' This is puzzling, yet we know it is true.

'Because they think their beliefs will keep them safe. But it's actually the opposite: fear and doubt lock the beliefs in place. What would happen, for example, if you let go of the fear that prevents you from experiencing yourself as Divine?'

We think for a moment. 'We might get a big head?'

The tree holds its middle, laughing. 'That would be a terrible result, wouldn't it? But actually, if you know yourself as Divine, what comes is a serene feeling of humility. Living from that place of Divine humility means living without judgment. More importantly, you will know *everything* as Divine.'

This idea is beginning to appeal to us. We try to imagine letting go of our constant judgments about what is good, better, best – and bad, worse, worst.

'What about #4 – us versus them?' asks the tree. 'The list of those who are better, more Divine, or closer to God. What do you think about that?'

'It's essentially the same thing, isn't it? If those people we see as special have spirit or Divinity in them – if they are Divine – then can't we be, also?'

The trees smiles. 'You have a fine mind. Believe what it is telling you now.'

We laugh.

'If you do, then you are home and free.'

'We wish it were that simple.'

The tree shakes its branches gently, its leaves fluttering. 'Ah, but it is.'

We take a deep breath, weighing the possibility.

'With Belief #4,' says the tree, 'the mind creates separation and judgment, putting oneself in the realm of opposites – good and evil, black and white, this and that. It's what you were taught, that certain people are the holy ones, and you are not. Some of *them* maintain the illusion as well, expecting others to revere and treat them differently. Some of the most respected, robed teachers on the planet keep the belief going by suggesting that epochs and eons will pass before awakening or enlightenment shows up for the rest of us. If we look at the essential truths of the major religions, however, we find that the torch bearers, those who light the way, tell us we are Divine.'

Let Go My Ego
We shift on the root seat, the better to see the tree. 'And what about the belief that we have work to do in the world, so it isn't desirable to experience oneself as Divine? We believe that. What *would* happen if everyone sat around meditating all the time? We wish to serve God, but not be God. We're afraid that if we spend too much time on spiritual pursuits, we will withdraw from the world, which needs our help.'

'That is a misconception,' says the tree. 'Many people fear that they will lose their motivation to be of service if they recognize themselves as Divine, but the opposite is true. As Divine beings, they will find themselves being servants of God. Their mere Presence brings about change in the world.'

'We can be Divine, and at the same time be of service to the Divine?'

'Yes. When you know your true essence as Divinity, your Presence will be a light to others, helping to dispel the darkness of their beliefs. The best way of *doing* in the world is *being* – there is no better or more powerful way to serve.'

We are silent, pondering. 'I just don't know if I can acknowledge myself as Divine.'

'You can when you are ready,' says the tree, 'and one day you will be. Could be today.' It winks. 'At this moment.'

'That's a hopeful thought,' we reply.

'That means you *wish* to believe it, which is very good. As in Belief #6, if you're unsure and are opening the door to discovering more, the best way is to close your eyes – *shut ye eyes in order to see* – and open up the possibilities.'

'You must mean going to the Well,' we say. 'That's a habit we'd like to establish once we return home.'

'It sounds as though you have had some insight into the reality of your Divinity and wish to experience more. Blessings will flow to you when you understand and know that *you* are the blessing.'

'It's true, we have had an inkling of our Divine nature.' We smile at the tree.

'One final thought,' says the tree. 'All of these are merely beliefs, and beliefs can be changed. By allowing the thought "Divinity is my true identity" into your mind and noticing what feelings, thoughts, and beliefs rise to the surface, you can allow the mind and body to reveal what keeps you from knowing this as Truth. Openness and humility – qualities you already have – these are the keys that will serve you well as you venture through the Isle of Is.'

*Each day for a week, pick up your **Wand** and write, 'Divinity is my true identity,' then write down any thoughts, feelings, or beliefs that point you away from that. Write at least one full page in your notebook, exploring your feelings and beliefs.*

*After writing, go to the **Well** for 15 minutes. Observe your thoughts and feelings. Do not judge the feelings; rather, embrace them with compassion and love.*

As we close our tablet and pack it into the quiver, we yawn and look up through the opening in the branches, surprised to see stars poking through.

The tree brings its lower limbs down to provide a cushion among the roots. 'The beliefs have been a heavy weight upon the body and the mind. Rest here among my roots. Be rooted here. Allow yourself to slumber. As you rest, let go of all concerns about the past and the future. There is just one reality to hold onto: Divinity is your true identity.'

We curl up in the curve of the root, nestling among the leaves. Soon we are fast asleep.

It is a restful sleep, without thoughts. When we awake, the morning sun is streaming down upon us. The briars have retreated, leaving a forested glen with parakeets and butterflies. During the night, our limiting beliefs have been dispelled.

We stand up and stretch. 'Thank you, dear tree, for being our teacher.'

'The pleasure is always mine,' says the tree. 'Peace to you as you go on your way.'

As we pick up the quiver, the map crackles. We hold it to the sun and see the trail being etched once more, out of the glen and into a meadow. A butterfly flits in front of us, mottled orange and white.

'We are to follow the butterfly, aren't we?' we say.

The tree smiles and closes its eyes, honoring our intuition.

*Take a few deep breaths. Let all these ideas be with you. Use the **Wand** and the **Well** as instructed earlier. Acknowledge your efforts and move on to the next chapter when you are ready.*

5 | The Ever-Present

A great silent space holds all of Nature in its embrace.
It also holds ye.

Eckhart Tolle

The butterfly weaves before us, creating a dazzling display. We feel uplifted by the grace of its flight. Along the way it pauses to smell the flowers, and we pause, too, grateful for the reminder. The sun shimmers through the upper branches of lantern trees and coral trees, filtering down around us to sparkle on ferns and grass.

Soon the path leads to a stream, where a bamboo footbridge stretches to the other bank. Bells tinkle nearby and we glance around, but see none. We look down. At our feet is the grandest array of bellflowers we've seen since visiting Auntie May's garden: royal waves, Bavarian blues, and white cup-and-saucers. Bellringers, with their pink and purple clusters. Starry sprays of blue waterfall tumbling over the rocks. And pantaloons, double tubular bells, where one purple bell grows right out of another. The flowers sway in the breeze, jingling once more. We smile at the idea that such flowers, known for their constancy and kindness, might actually chime.

The butterfly is crossing the bridge, and we follow her lead. In the center of the bridge we stop to watch the stream splashing over rocks and tree roots on its journey toward the sea. Remembering our experience in the briar, we visualize our outmoded beliefs being carried downstream. A lightness comes, as though we have taken off a heavy garment; inside, we feel a new spaciousness.

On the opposite bank is a sign with an arrow that points straight ahead and the accompanying words, "To Be." Here the trail enters more forest, lushly green. A few minutes later we spy a meadow that opens bright in the sun. As we near the clearing, our butterfly guide flits ahead to join other butterflies engaged in a communal dance.

At the edge of the forest, in the center of the path, is a stump upon which words are carved:

> <   **Leave Here the Past**
> **Leave Here the Future**   >

To the left of the trail, situated in the forest, is a large basket woven of thick leaves. To the right sits another just like it.

We pause to honor this request, closing our eyes and asking that all thoughts, feelings, and concerns associated with the past be deposited in the basket to our left. When we open our eyes, we are astonished to see the basket filling up with crumpled paper, emotional rubbish, worn photographs, tissues wet with spent tears, and tarnished items that fill our garage back home. Watching this makes us laugh. So this is what the past looks like!

So this is what the past looks like.

And what of the future? Surely there is not so much stuff. We close our eyes again and ask that all thoughts, feelings, plans, and worries about the future be released from us and placed in the basket to our right. After a few moments, we venture a peek. The basket is piled high with a brochure for the new car we can't afford, worry about who will win the next election, an article on global warming, unused rolls of film meant for photos of future grandchildren, our biological clock ticking, fear that we might not outlive our retirement plan, and unfinished projects on our desk calendar at work.

It's unsettling to see all these things we have been carrying around with us. We wonder, what must life be like without them?

As we are about to enter the meadow, we check to see whether we have an appropriate key. Indeed, the ring holds a key carved with the image of a grassy meadow, with insects and butterflies flying about. In our hand the key begins to vibrate and pulse with a soft yellow light. Then, a thought, *We do not need the key – we are already here.* We honor the thought, placing the ring of keys back in the quiver.

About a quarter of a mile in diameter, the meadow is surrounded on all sides by forest. What will we discover here?

We have just entered the meadow when the base of a rainbow begins to form at the far left edge of the clearing. It materializes slowly, as though an artist were painting each band of color with long smooth strokes. Gradually the rainbow forms an arch over the meadow, culminating at the far right. Its hues are iridescent.

We hold up the map. Yes, a rainbow now shows on the map. As we study the map, the image of the meadow is emblazoned with light. We glance up to see light pouring down beyond the rainbow, illuminating the space all around.

Tucking the map away, we take a deep breath. Now we know our destination: the light beyond the rainbow. Slowly we walk across the meadow and through the rainbow to where the light filters down.

The air changes as we enter the light. It is warm and tingly on our skin. We stand immersed in this radiance for a long time, breathing in the aliveness, feeling ourselves fully in the light, both within and without.

Set aside all concerns about past and future.

Meditation in the Ever-Present: *You are about to enter a sacred meditation. Read these instructions first, then enter the **Well**, where you will remain in silence for 20 to 30 minutes.*

You will close your eyes and visualize yourself on a path in a forest. In front of you is a meadow. Before you enter the meadow, you pause at the edge of the forest to set down all concerns and attachments to the past and future.

See yourself turning to your left and placing in a basket all feelings, thoughts, and concerns about the past, all painful experiences and worries from the past. As more thoughts or feelings about the past come to you, allow them to be placed in the basket beside you. Take a few moments to do this.

Then turn to your right and place in a second basket all thoughts, feelings, plans, and worries about the future. Take a few moments to release all concerns about the future. Know that you can always come back and pick up anything you have placed in the baskets. For now, allow them to rest here at the edge of the forest.

See yourself standing taller and lighter now that you have released the past and future. Then step into the meadow.

Before you a rainbow forms an arch over the meadow. Beyond the rainbow is a brilliant golden light that beckons you to come . . . to immerse yourself in its luminescence. Walk across the meadow and through the arch.

Once through the arch, allow yourself to feel the light. Feel it on your skin. Breathe it into your body. Visualize and feel it as it fills every cell of your body.

Remain in silence for 20 to 30 minutes. If thoughts come to you, do not push them away. Rather, gently bring your awareness back to the light and the sensation of light in your body. Allow yourself to feel the light, feel the energy, in all the cells of your body, from the top of your head to the tips of your toes. Know that this light is you – this energy is you – this is the truth of who you are.

Now . . . enter the silence of the Meditation.

CD Track 2:

The Ever-Present

At the end of the Meditation, slowly open your eyes. Take a few moments to sit quietly with your eyes open. Look around you. What do you notice? Take out your Wand and write about your experience, using free writing to describe any images or feelings that have come. Place no judgment on what you experienced. Do not label it as good or bad. Merely write about your experience.

In this meditation, the cells of the body can feel deeply alive, and you can experience a shift in awareness. This may happen the first time you enter the Meditation in the Ever-Present, or on subsequent occasions. The power of the Meditation is twofold:

• First, in setting aside all concerns about past and future, you are able to come into the Ever-Present, which is where Divinity resides. Past and future do not exist here.

- Second, by allowing yourself to be immersed in light, an experience of Divine Presence (also called Presence or Being) may wash over and through you. This Presence or Being is always accessible. It is not a product of the illusion of the mind. It is true reality.

These two aspects – setting aside past and future, and visualizing being immersed in light – are crucial to this meditation and others you will experience in later chapters. The meadow is a metaphor for the Ever-Present; the light represents the Presence or quality of Divinity that resides there.

This Is Heaven, Man

We decide to sit in the shade to gather our thoughts and feelings. Near the edge of the meadow an almond tree – a tavola – branches out over a small brook, making a perfect resting place. We take off our shoes to feel the grass between our toes and duck under the branches so that we can sit under the tree and lean against its trunk.

The experience we have just had at the Well is familiar to us. It is a feeling of timelessness, as though there is no past or future. Perhaps we have been living in the past-future dimension and have forgotten this experience. In the past-future, we weigh and measure most aspects of our daily life in relationship to time. What time is it? Do we have enough time? Are we on time? We worry about all manner of things that are past and feel the residue of past experiences in our daily lives, as though the past were tugging at us with strong, invisible fingers. As well, we are concerned about what lies ahead for us – next year, next month, next moment! We live so little of our life in the present that no time is left for Now.

As we think these thoughts, a caterpillar crawls to the very tip of a leaf before our eyes. We gaze at it intently and see that it is looking back at us. 'Who are you?' we ask.

'I am Conscious Caterpillar. You may call me Connie. And who are you?'

'A traveler on the Isle of Is.'

'It's grand, isn't it?' Connie says.

'It is wonderful,' we agree.

'I saw you standing under the rainbow and thought you might have a question or two. Most humans do.'

We are baffled by the appearance of a talking caterpillar, one that can answer philosophical questions at that.

The caterpillar cocks her head knowingly. 'Suspend judgment,' she says, wagging a leg in our direction. 'Even this question will be answered here.'

'You know what we're thinking!'

Connie waggles her antennae, smiling.

'We were wondering about time, which seemed to disappear while we stood in the light. What happened just now?'

Lifting herself to face us, Connie stands on her 12 back legs. 'You know about *my* life, don't you? That I am a caterpillar-butterfly?'

We nod. 'Yes, we do.'

'Even though what you see in front of you has many legs and no wings, I am already a butterfly in my heart. I'm not involved in worry about metamorphosis. What will happen tomorrow is none of my concern.'

'This is true for all of us,' says a wee voice beside her.

On a neighboring leaf is a shiny red bug with black legs and antennae and a sporty black vest.

'Hello,' we say, astonished.

'Hello to you, too,' says the bug. 'Pleased to meet you. Like Connie, we are all expressions of the Ever-Present. They honor my buddhahood by calling me Buda Bug. Lucky me.' He winks. 'Occasionally I play lead bass for our local band, Buda and the 'Hood.'

We cannot suppress a laugh, which sends Buda tumbling on his leaf.

'Enjoying the Ever-Present is beyond most humans' experience,' Connie says. 'The rest of us are in a joyous state in the Ever-Present. We live in this place and are not subject to time. We live in accord with this unification you call Nature. Everywhere we go, it *is*.'

Buda chuckles. 'Yeah, this is Heaven, man.'

Connie tilts her head, her antennae bobbing. 'It really puzzles us to see humans not getting it, not understanding. How do you get so attached to your thoughts and your mind?'

We ponder this. Why *do* we get so attached to our thoughts? We get caught up in what's happening around us, and we forget to reflect or be in Nature.

'Ah, so you forget,' Connie says before we can answer, nodding to the red bug.

'How can you forget?' says Buda. 'It's right in front of your very noses.'

We laugh in amazement, as the leaves in front of us fill up with other bugs and caterpillars, kingfishers, lorikeets – even our Ever-Present guide, the butterfly.

'And we suppose you all talk?' we ask.

'Aye. Yes. Yeah, man,' chimes a chorus of tiny voices.

The butterfly waves her wings at us. 'Hello to you,' she says. 'Let me introduce myself. I'm Netti-Netti Butterfly. In Hindi my name means "not this, not that." Some also call me Butterfly Netti, because I catch travelers and bring them to the Ever-Present.'

Netti turns to the others. 'This traveler has just come from the Briar,' she explains.

'Oh. Ooo. Ah,' they say. 'The old Sentinel of the Briar is a fine teacher,' says one.

Netti turns back to us. 'Most human children, when they are born, start out life more like us. They love Nature and being outdoors. They delight in every single moment, until they need something that is not provided for them, like food or water or a hug or a comfortable place to sleep. It is their surroundings – their families, schools, friends – that teach them to move away from the Ever-Present.'

'We know what you are speaking of. It's a terrible shame,' we say.

All nod in agreement.

Connie looks at us intently. 'One of the prophets in your realm said that unless you become like a child, you cannot enter the kingdom of Heaven.'

'And the kingdom of Heaven is the Ever-Present? This place where you enjoy every single thing?' we ask.

Wherever you are is where Heaven is.

Connie clasps two legs in front of her. 'Yes. Heaven is really everywhere, which is why we call it the Ever-Present. Wherever you are is where Heaven is, but it's a matter of realizing it. Here inside the Ever-Present, we experience the unity of all things.'

'We can see why you call this the Ever-Present,' we exclaim. 'It is always here, isn't it? But we never thought of insects as being Divine creatures.'

'We are Divinity in its myriad forms,' says Connie. 'Everything is alive. Everything has a voice. We are merely aspects of the creative, intelligent energy that pervades all matter and space. The indigenous peoples of the world know this: We Divine creatures show up in the folk tales and stories of Africa, Asia, Australia, New Zealand, the Americas, and the Celts and Slavic peoples of Europe.'

Connie dips her head toward us. 'You're surprised that we talk, aren't you?'

'Yes! Most people would say it's impossible. Some would even say that we're crazy to be talking to you!'

'Then we'll show you a story,' says Connie. 'A true story of a human from your world who visits Nature in the Ever-Present.'

The shade under the tree becomes darker, as though the lights in a theater are growing dim. A story begins to play, like a hologram, in the space between where we are sitting and the rows of seats – the leaves – for the creatures on the tree.

Rachel and her sister Leah share a brick house on the edge of a small city. The two of them enjoy watching birds, so they buy a bird feeder and mount it outside their kitchen window.

Shortly thereafter, Rachel visits the Isle of Is. Her experiences on the island increase her interest in communing with Nature's creatures. When she returns home, she sits on the deck and speaks to the birds when they visit the feeder. 'Hello, pretty bird. Will you come talk to me?' she says.

Several of the birds begin to perch on a fence near where she sits and cock their heads to listen. Leah comments on the change in the birds' behavior.

During the next few months, Rachel makes friends with several of the birds. One, a blue jay, breaks his wing in a fall and hops to the doorstep, dragging the wing. Once at the door, he calls Rachel for help. Rachel and Leah put the blue jay in a box and take him to a refuge for birds, where a veterinarian sets his wing. In a few weeks, he is able to fly again.

Another bird, a small hawk that does not eat at the feeder, comes to a tree branch over Rachel's head whenever she calls the birds. Soon, Rachel calls him specifically, and he responds to her call. The goshawk stays as long as Rachel is outside. When she goes inside, he flies away. Sometimes the goshawk will squeak to let Rachel know he is nearby, then fly to a branch where she can see him. Then Rachel goes outside to be present with him.

'This is true?' we ask as the story fades. 'Is it really possible? Or must one have a special gift to be able to speak with animals, like St Francis of Assisi?'

'Oh, we are eager and waiting,' says Netti, her wings fluttering in the breeze. 'If you still your mind and have the intention of communicating with us, we are right here waiting for you. When you begin to visit the Ever-Present in an ongoing way, you will experience and know all possibilities. It is an understanding that comes.'

'We like it when you acknowledge and speak to us.' Connie's caterpillar face is glowing. 'Nature comes to know its own sacredness and beauty through you. This is truth.'

Weight-Lifting the Veil
Buda Bug flies off his leaf and makes loops in front of us before landing on our finger. 'In your realm,' Buda says, settling his wings, 'cool things happen, and humans forget to tell the stories to their children, to keep the stories alive.'

'Without which,' Connie adds, 'much wisdom is lost.'

Buda smiles at her assistance. 'In one of these stories that happened long ago, a young mother took her wee one with her on an outing. She was driving an automobile, with her baby in a basket beside her, when one of the tires went flat. She had to pull over on a steep hill and stop the car. No one was around to help, so she set the baby in its basket beside the car and proceeded to change the tire. Suddenly the car began to roll in the direction of the baby. With one arm the woman held the 2000-pound vehicle, while she grabbed the baby with the other arm, preventing the car from crushing the baby.'

'Ooooh,' say the bugs in unison. 'Good story.'

'How was she able to do that?' we ask.

'By being in the Ever-Present,' says Buda. 'The crisis brought her awareness totally into the present, and that allowed her to tap into the great power that resides there.'

'But there is more to this story,' Netti says. 'That woman was your grandmother, and the baby was your mother. Her destiny was to give birth to you. You see how Spirit, working through the Ever-Present, intervened in your family's lives.'

It is an awesome thought. We are surprised that Mother never told us the story, and we suspect that Grandma never told it to Mother. Grandma missed the opportunity to pass on her experience and her connection to Divinity. Grandma was never one to boast about her accomplishments; she just did what needed to be done and didn't talk much about it. But we find that this story means a great deal to us, knowing that Spirit made sure our mother – and we – could live.

'Here is another example from your own life,' Connie says, 'which your grandmother's story inspired in someone else. This is the story of Samuel Jones, the man who delivers your mail back home. His parents read about "wonder woman and the wobbling wheel" in the newspaper and told the story to Samuel when he was a boy. Samuel, of course, does not know the story involves you and has never told you about his own experiences when he was 17 years old.'

We have always liked Mr Jones, but we've never asked him about his youth. The shade under the tree darkens again as another story begins to play:

Unusual for most teenagers, Samuel Jones has lived his life in the Ever-Present and thus knows that the possibilities are limitless. Samuel is on the middleweight weightlifting team in high school. At 5'9" tall and 172 pounds, he is one of the smallest on the team.

This particular afternoon students form small groups in order to practice their lifts. As he watches others lifting, Samuel wishes to prove a point to them about the arbitrary limits they have set for themselves. So when it is his turn, he sets about placing as much weight on the bar as will fit. He and his partners start taking all the weights away from the other groups to set up for this one lift. When the clanging stops, it adds up to 1000 pounds. To everyone except Samuel, that amount of weight seems beyond possibility. At his age and weight, a dead lift of 350 pounds would be spectacular.

The commotion of bringing all the weights over has created additional interest from the others in the gym. The students and coaches gather around. Samuel draws upon the energy of their presence to assist in the lift. He takes several breaths of concentration, feeling the flow of the Ever-Present coursing through his body and tapping into the others who are present. Amidst much cheering – and breaking the barriers of belief – Samuel is able to gradually pull the weight off the floor to its completion. As he lets the weights flow from his fingers and clang heavily on the floor, he knows he has made the point. He has sent home the message of opening the field of possibilities.

The light returns, and Buda Bug speaks. 'Within days the other lifters had also increased their own weights beyond what they could formerly lift.'

'Was that a record? One thousand pounds for his size?'

'It was,' says Buda, a grin on his tiny face. 'Neat, huh? This is a story of a human living in the Ever-Present. Such events happen in your world. You have heard of them or perhaps experienced them yourself. They are not uncommon, but they are often dismissed.'

An incident comes to mind that occurred when we were a young adult, in the early 1980s, and we are excited to tell it. 'We were bathing in a tub of water when an electric hair dryer that was plugged into the wall fell in. The electricity flowing through the water should have disabled our muscles and would have killed us, but we were able to pick up the dryer and throw it out of the tub. Everyone said it was impossible to do that.'

'It's a good example,' says Buda. 'The energy of the Ever-Present was available to you. Some cultures would call this supernatural, as though it were outside Nature. But it is actually what Nature is all about.'

We think about Samuel, who is always kind and never gets upset about anything. 'What about Samuel? The story said he lives in the Ever-Present.'

'He does,' says Netti. 'He is so immersed there that he finds no need to boast or constantly tell people about it. He enjoys the peace and the silence, but his mere presence makes him as an emissary of the Ever-Present. Samuel delivers more than mail.'

'Is it possible to live one's life like that? Being in the meadow is the way we think Heaven might be, that feeling of peace and joy. But to be there all the time . . . ?'

'What now seems miraculous is meant to be commonplace,' says Connie.

'Like metamorphosis?' we ask.

Connie's eyes dance. 'Yes, like metamorphosis.'

Netti flitters to a nearby leaf. 'Metamorphosis is transformation, you know.'

We nod. 'Yes, we know.'

'It is also about remaining in the Divine essence of a thing, in its heart, regardless of the changing aspects of the material world. It is a wonderful word for what happens on the island.'

'So *we* may also have a metamorphosis?' we ask.

'Exactly, the Isle places you in the middle of that – a metamorphosis of knowing and understanding,' says Netti.

Buda Bug buzzes in front of us. 'Hey, before you leave, little traveler, the 'Hood and I would like to do a number for you. One of our favorite routines.'

'That would be great fun!' We glance around to see if we can identify the bugs in the 'Hood. Sure enough, four red-and-black bugs lift off neighboring leaves and gather around Buda.

'A tip to you,' Buda says to us. 'Notice the silence between the words and inside the music. Without the silence, there would be no music. Okay. Ready, guys? A-one-and-a-two-and-a . . . '

Without the silence, there would be no music.

'Buddha in the 'hood,' they chant, snapping their front legs together. Then pause.

'Buddha in the 'hood.' A longer pause.

'Buddha in the 'hood.' And then silence.

We want to laugh at the simplicity of the song and the sight of five bugs rocking out on the tavola tree. But we hold the laughter inside and wait. All the creatures are silent, as though they are resting.

Finally Buda speaks. 'Silence is one of the qualities of the Ever-Present. It is always there, behind the words and behind the notes of music. Just as space is always there, whether you fill it up with furniture or not.'

'Notice the silence and the space,' says Connie. 'These will take you to the Ever-Present any time you wish, because these exist in the Ever-Present – or the Field, as some humans call it.'

'Oh,' we say, then realize that the meadow is the Field!

'Traveler, do you understand the lyrics of the song?' asks Netti.

'Not really.' We shake our head. 'We were about to ask Buda.'

Buda takes off his dark glasses. 'Buddha is a name that means the illuminated one. Like me.' His face beams love and peace. 'And the 'hood, well, that refers to being a light in your own backyard, your own neighborhood, wherever it is that you live. The song is about infusing pure spirit into the physical world and jiving on every minute of it. Us bugs, we rejoice in that, even with this simple song. It doesn't need another verse.'

'Before you leave, go back and revisit the meadow.' Netti waves one wing toward the center of the field. 'To the place where the light pours down. Allow the light to fill you with its Divine energy. This will prepare you for the next stage on your journey – and for the rest of your life.'

'Thank you for your help,' we say, smiling at each and every creature. 'You have been wonderful company in the Ever-Present. We have learned so much. We see that living in the Ever-Present is meant to be playful and fun, not so serious as we've always thought.'

Netti bows her head, honoring *us*.

'Thank you, thank you,' the others say, waving goodbye.

We stand and shoulder our quiver, ready to return to the meadow.

'Happy metamorphosis!' calls Connie.

Living in the Ever-Present is meant to be playful and fun.

CD Track 2:

The Ever-Present

*Visit the **Meditation in the Ever-Present** often. Today begin a daily practice. Twice a day is best, for 20 to 30 minutes at a time. Do this for at least a week, and until you receive further instructions. In a short while, you will live there always.*

6 | *The Waves of Energy*

The Force be with Ye.

> Obe Wan Kinobe

The Force BE ye. Ye are the Force.

> Captain of the Boat E. Satva

A feeling of deep peace suffuses our being. The light of the meadow envelops us in its sunny warmth, yet we know we have other places to go on the island. Many keys still wait on the ring.

We sense that we are to walk across the meadow, to the forest that is directly ahead of us. We reach the edge of the field quickly, but no path is obvious, so we take the keys in our hands once more, asking for guidance about the next step. One of the keys vibrates – the key that is carved with waves and rocks. Still, no pathway opens. We hold the map to the sun, which begins to etch a path into the forest. Glancing around for a clue about where to enter, we find none. We examine trees and bushes, touch the earth with our foot, feeling around for a stone or a magic button.

We remember the instruction, *Close your eyes that ye might see.* When we do so, we feel it: a pulsating that seems to emanate from one particular tree. We run our fingers along the trunk, which is nubby. Ah, here it is! A keyhole carved into ridges in the bark.

With the key inserted into the tree trunk, a space opens between two bushes, and a trail emerges, two feet wide. We hold out the key. 'Make more space,' we say, and the bushes retreat even further, so that there is plenty of room for us to walk. We are amazed with how we are following our intuition and asking for what nurtures us, and that Nature is responding.

The trail meanders through sprawling shrubs, tufted grasses, and acacia trees laced with pea vines. We are definitely traveling to a different part of the island. With each step, we are very much in touch with Nature – feeling, seeing, sensing. Whereas before we were intent on getting to the next location on the island, this time we are enjoying every moment. Before visiting the meadow, our mind was involved with many thoughts; now we are in a greater place of peace and joy.

To our left, we see a solitary plant waving in the breeze, although everything around it is quite still. We smile. Is a small draft of wind grazing the plant? Or is it trying to get our attention? A little further along the trail, we see another plant waving. We wave back.

'Hello-o-o-o!' the plant calls. 'It's a joy to see you.'

How could we have ever, in our life, felt alone?

'Hello!' we call back. This communing with the plants heightens our delight even further. How could we have ever, in our life, felt alone?

Still further along, we spot a green snake sunning itself on a tree branch. As we approach, it turns its head toward us lazily. When we wave, it flicks its tail in response.

We have learned from the creatures in the Ever-Present about the unity of all things. Now we are beginning to have that experience on this 'everyday walk of life.'

The air has a salty smell, and we sense we are nearing the sea. Indeed, the trail opens out onto a rock cropping with low-lying brush, a promontory that overlooks the ocean. This side of the island is more rugged than the area where we disembarked. On the promontory are several large stones, standing watch as though they were left here by an ancient civilization. Two of them are several feet in height; a third is flat and round. They greet us with their Presence, and we pause before them, in awe of their grandeur.

Setting down our quiver, we walk to the edge of the cliff. Below are a pebbly beach, rocks wet with foam, and waves that dance and splash all about.

Wind

The breeze that wafts up from the ocean feels enlivening after our long walk. We take a deep breath, filling our lungs with the pure, clear air. Once, we thought of air as a void, but now we know it as nurturing and alive. The particles of air have life in them. The breeze comes and goes in a rhythm, very much like our own breath.

We lift our arms to acknowledge the nurturing breeze, raising our hands to the sky in gratitude. Within moments we are filled with something more – waves of energy. Our fingertips and palms tingle and grow warm as we receive the energy of the heavens.

This energy – called *prana* in India, *qi* (chi) in China, *ki* in Japan and Korea – seems to come out of nowhere (the Ever-Present) when we stand in the chalice pose. Our outreached hands call in the energy that surrounds us, inviting it to move through us and mingle with our own.

The Chalice. *Stand with your feet a little wider than shoulder width apart, toes pointed slightly inward, your hands at your sides. Relax the knees, tuck the buttocks under, and lift the sternum. Relax the shoulders and look gently straight ahead. Visualize and allow yourself to feel the energy of the Earth coming up through the soles of your feet into your ankles, rising into your calves and shins, your thighs, and up into your torso. Stand in this pose for two or three minutes. Relax deeply, and allow your mind to be calm and still.*

Inhaling, begin to raise the arms slowly outward to the sides, away from the body. Continue to raise them until they are overhead, forming a chalice with your body. Relax into this posture. Visualize and allow yourself to feel the energy of the heavens coming down through your hands and arms, into your shoulders and torso. Visualize the energies of Heaven and Earth mingling in your body.

Breathe.

Relax your shoulders while keeping the arms upraised. Allow yourself to feel tingling or warmth in your hands – this is the energy that fills and surrounds your body. Remain in this position for a couple of minutes.

Very slowly allow the arms to descend once more. Bring the fingertips to meet in front of the navel. Remain still and at peace in this position for four or five more minutes.

When we have completed the pose, we feel calm and relaxed – centered. Looking around, we allow ourselves to see things with new eyes. There is an extra intensity to the light. Before, it was merely daylight. Now the colors are more lucid and contain a certain sweetness.

Modern science confirms the existence of the energy that is in and around our bodies. Electromagnetic fields pervade and surround everything, from the insects on the leaves of the trees, to the air we breathe and the gravel beneath our feet. We are truly one unified force field, the energy of each thing touching and overlapping the next. Although invisible to the naked eye, energy is everywhere.

The chalice pose gives us an opportunity to connect with the forces of Heaven and Earth. It is a beautiful way to start each day.

The chalice of Christ's Last Supper – the Holy Grail – is a symbol of Divine consciousness, of being aware of the Divinity in all things. Just as the Knights of the Round Table sought the chalice outside themselves and traveled far outside the kingdom in their search, we may be tempted to look outside ourselves for fulfillment, wholeness, and completeness.

Eventually the knight Gawain realized that the grail was within. The spiritual teacher Meister Eckhardt affirms that the knights' search was indeed an inward search. He equates the search for the grail with the development of conscious awareness – awareness of one's own Divinity.

We can know our place among all creation.

We, too, can know that the grail is within, using the chalice pose to remind us of our Divinity. By connecting with the heavens and the Earth, the wind and the rock, we can know our place among all creation.

Rock

'Hey, over here!' says a low voice.

We look around but see no one. No bugs, either – no flowers or mushrooms or trees.

'Down here.'

There is nothing on the ground but rocks, dry shrubs, and pieces of coral from the reefs.

'The rock!' rumbles the voice. We look intently at a smooth rock, the lowest and flattest of the standing stones, situated a few feet from the edge of the cliff. The voice seems to emanate from there.

'You? Rock?' we ask awkwardly. We don't know how to address a rock.

'Yes, me, rock. I have energy, too. Come closer and touch my surface with your hands.'

We place both hands on the rock.

'Feel anything?' says the rock.

We close our eyes, skeptical. But, wait a minute – we do feel something. 'There's a low vibration,' we say. 'It's very subtle. Is that what you mean?'

'Yes, that's me, alright.'

'But we thought you were an inanimate object.'

'Ha! You see. Your schooling misleads you. I am animate, but my vibration is much lower and beyond your normal realm of perception. I am alive in my own way.' The rock is silent for a few moments. 'Come. Sit on me. Allow yourself to be comfortable. I wish to show you something.'

We sit on the rock. 'Are we too heavy?'

The rock chortles. 'Not too heavy for a rock. But very soon you will feel your own density. Please place your hands on your thighs.'

We situate ourselves so that we can oblige.

'Close your eyes, please. Now, very, very slowly, raise your hands up away from your thighs, toward the sky. So slowly that if someone were watching, they might not see the movement.'

As we lift our hands, they feel surprisingly heavy.

'Take your time,' says the rock. 'What is time, anyway, in the Ever-Present?'

We raise our hands as slowly as we can. It's a strange feeling, as they vibrate a little with the upward movement.

'When your hands are at chest height,' continues the rock, 'slowly turn them so that the palms face each other, and gradually begin to move them toward each other. When you have brought them close together, without touching, slowly move them apart again.'

As we turn our wrists, the muscles jerk slightly. It is not as smooth as we thought it might be. We had not noticed before the effect of making such tiny movements. The palms of our hands have grown warm. 'What is this feeling?' we ask. 'The prickly feeling in the tips of our fingers? And this thick stuff we feel between our hands. It's like pulling taffy!'

'This is energy – your energy,' says the rock. 'You are feeling the energy of the Universe flowing through you.'

CD Track 3:

Prana Exercise

Prana Exercise. *Sit in a chair with your feet flat on the floor, your hands relaxed, palms on your thighs. Close your eyes and take a few deep relaxed breaths. If you feel tension in your body, sit quietly for a few minutes with your awareness on the breath. Breathe, and relax.*

When you are ready, begin by lifting the weight of your hands off your thighs, so that the fingertips are still touching the thighs ever so lightly. Bring your awareness to the sensations in your fingertips and the palms of your hands.

Then slowly raise the hands off the thighs, so slowly that it is almost imperceptible to the eye. Take a few minutes to do this. The more slowly you move, the more benefit you will feel from this exercise. Breathe, and be aware of the sensations in your hands.

When your hands are at chest height, slowly turn them so that the palms are facing each other. Then begin to move the palms toward each other, with your eyes still closed. Take a couple of minutes to do this. When the palms are quite close, move them apart again, very slowly.

Play with the hand movements: Move the hands together and apart more quickly, like an accordion. Then visualize yourself holding a ball between your hands. Allow your hands to rotate, feeling the outer edges of the ball, as you keep the palms facing each other.

Move the hands apart once more, returning them to chest height, and turn them so they are facing down. Let the hands drift slowly down to your thighs.

Bring your awareness once more to the breath, and slowly open your eyes.

Take out your **Wand** *and record your experience. What sensations did you feel?*

One thing we notice is the feeling of calmness that comes with doing this exercise. We wonder why this is so.

'You are calmer,' says the rock, 'because in this exercise you have visited the Ever-Present. The Ever-Present is full of that essence that some call "Presence," "prana," or "chi." It is not empty space. It has qualities that you can feel – qualities of peace and joy and love. It is a field of feeling. You have tapped into the electromagnetic field that surrounds the human body, as well as the life force, or spirit, within.'

We are amazed that we could feel it. 'Do you feel it, too?' we ask the rock.

'Oh, yes. I feel it in my rock self. It is what I am. This energy – Divine energy – is who we *all* really are.'

'These ideas are very new to us,' we say, trying to understand our experiences, to make sense of them with our mind. 'Are electromagnetic fields really everywhere?'

'Yes. The same force embraces all the rocks – the Earth, the planets, the stars. It affects the movement of the celestial bodies.'

'But isn't the space between the planets empty? At least, that is what we were taught.'

'No,' says the rock. 'Space is not empty. It too is filled with Divine energy.'

'Amazing,' we say. These ideas are challenging many of our cherished beliefs.

Our ears pick up the sound of the waves as they tumble onto the rocks below. We turn to see spumes of white foam lift into the air.

'Oh, yes, and those rocks, too,' says the rock. 'My cousins get to play in the water all day long. And lucky me, I get to watch them!'

Water

Our senses have felt the waves of the wind, the vibration of a rock, and now the energy in our own hands. And the rock has assured us that even space is not empty. It appears that there is life force in everything.

The ocean waves beckon us. We stand and walk to the cliff's edge to get a better view of the water, rocks, and beach below. The force of the waves seems to touch us, even at this distance. Such power they carry with them!

We know it is time to go. Bidding adieu to the rock, we examine the side of the cliff, where we discover a stone path down the escarpment. Minutes later, our shoes full of gravel, we stand on a narrow ribbon of beach that curves out of sight to the left. We empty our shoes and walk barefoot to the water's edge.

Our journey has brought us to this auspicious moment. We sense that something wonderful awaits us here. We feel it in the spilling and churning of the surf. *Show us*, we say silently, inviting whoever or whatever is here to present itself. We stand quietly and wait.

Soon we hear it – the voices in the waves. It is an ocean of beings! Indistinguishable from one another at first, the voices begin to separate into messages of endearment. 'Dear one,' says one. 'Sweetness,' says another. 'Love incarnate,' says a third.

Our heart opens as we receive message after message, knowing that they are speaking to us.

As we peer out to sea, a big wave, grander than the rest, begins to make its way to shore. This is the Big Kahuna! We have heard this term before, which refers to the wave that surpasses all others. Its name means 'giver of secrets.' We wonder what secret it is carrying for us. Could there be anything grander than what we have already received from the other waves?

This energy you feel – this is the presence of the Divine.

'You know our secret,' says the wave as it nears the shore. 'Divinity is in everything, and especially in you. This energy you feel – this is the presence of the Divine.'

We laugh. There is a theme on the island, is there not?

As the Big Kahuna crashes onto the rocks, all the voices come together as a choir, an ensemble. 'Be still,' they say, 'and listen to our words.'

CD Track 4:

Divine Personalities

Meditation with Divine Personalities. *You are about to enter the* **Well** *through a meditation that will give you an experience of the Divine qualities of energy.*

Sit comfortably in a chair or on a rock, feet on the floor or ground, spine erect. Close your eyes and bring your awareness to your breath. Simply observe the breath coming in and going out. Be present with your breath for a few minutes. If thoughts intercede, gently bring your awareness back to the breath.

Now visualize yourself on a path in a forest. Ahead of you is a glorious meadow. But before you enter the meadow, you will stop at the edge of the forest and set down everything associated with the past and future. Place past concerns in a basket to the left, and future concerns in a basket to the right. Take as much time as you need to do this.

When you have finished, see yourself standing taller and lighter, facing the meadow. Step into the meadow. Before you is a rainbow, through which shines a brilliant golden white light. Walk to the rainbow and step through to the other side. Enter the light.

Feel the light on your skin. Breathe it into your lungs. Visualize it spreading to every cell in your body. Take a few moments to do this.

Now look ahead of you, into the light. As you do, a figure comes into view. This figure begins to walk toward you. It is the figure of the one known as Jesus. He approaches you and stands before you. Allow yourself to feel his energy – the energy of his love, his peace.

When you can feel this energy, he steps aside.

In front of you, another figure comes into view. This figure walks toward you. It is the one known as Buddha, the illumined one. He too comes forth and stands before you in order for you to feel his energy – the energy of his peace, his illumination. Allow yourself to feel this.

When you can feel this energy, he also steps aside.

A third figure begins to form in front of you. It walks toward you, and you see that it is Mother – perhaps the Divine Mother, Mother Mary, Mother Teresa, or Mother Earth. She comes and stands before you. Allow yourself to feel the energy of her compassion, devotion, and love. Take a few moments to do this.

Yet a fourth figure begins to walk toward you. This is a Divine personality that you draw to you – it might be Shiva, Saraswati, Kuan Yin, Sophia the goddess of wisdom, Mohammed, or some other Divine being. Allow yourself to recognize the being that approaches you. This one comes before you to allow you to feel their energy.

This being joins the other three, who take hands and form a circle around you. For the next 20 to 30 minutes, allow yourself to be in their energy, surrounded by their love.

When you are ready, slowly open your eyes.

When we have finished, we rest in the sensations of the experience. The waves have grown quieter and are beginning to recede, leaving us alone with our thoughts and feelings. We wish to record our experience.

*With your **Wand** free-write about your experience. Were there different qualities for each of the Divine personalities? Were there similarities? How did you feel, and what did you feel?*

By inviting the presence of Divine personalities, we can expand our experience and knowing of what Divinity feels like. Repeated sensory experiences of the Divine – feelings of fullness, tenderness, serenity, and joy – enable us to call forth the sensations whenever we wish. We learn what it feels like, and how to call it to us. The quality of our moments begins to grow until we are spending all our time in Divine Presence.

This is the purpose of the Meditation with Divine Personalities. Repeated experiences with this meditation will provide you with a grounding in the feeling of Divinity and Divine energy.

Fire

We decide to walk along the water's edge and think about our experiences. The messages of the waves continue to resound inside us: *Dear One . . . Sweetness . . . Love Incarnate.* 'Thank you, thank you,' we say to the waves. 'Thank you, Jesus, Buddha, Mother, for visiting me here.' We find ourselves overwhelmed with the desire to flow back what we are receiving. It is like a fire that burns in our heart.

We have received energy in a myriad of forms. We can also send it out to the world, thus completing the cycle by participating in the flow of love that animates all life. Just like the rays of the sun's light, we too can radiate beams of love.

We wonder what might be the impact of flowing it back. What, if anything, changes when we participate in this cycle? We pick up a small rock and skim it across the water. Does skimming the rock change anything? We watch as ripples ever-widen from the points where the rock touched the surface of the water.

We think of Anna, whose face shone with light after her visit to the Isle of Is. The waves of energy obviously touched her. Before we came, Anna showed us a book called *Messages from Water* by Masaru Emoto, a Japanese scientist who studied the impact of one's thoughts on the molecular structure of water. He found that crystals of water change when someone prays over it, plays it classical music, or even exposes it to words such as 'thank you' or 'I love you.' The book seemed unbelievable to us at the time. Now we feel open to these ideas.

Thoughts of home come to us . . . of Auntie May undergoing surgery soon . . . of our neighbor taking his exam to become a paramedic . . . of Samuel Jones, our mailman, whose teenage son has dropped out of school. If our thoughts and emotions can have such a powerful impact on water, what must be the impact of our love on those around us? We stop by the water's edge and seat ourselves on the sand. Closing our eyes, we send love to all these people, visualizing our thoughts traveling across the ocean on waves of energy to our neighborhood back home.

What must be the impact of our love on those around us?

On a fresh page, list people, pets, other elements of Nature, and situations to which you wish to send your love. Take a few minutes to do this. The list might contain a few items, or many.

Once you have finished the list, close your eyes and ask that your loving energy be sent to all these people and situations. Visualize this love traveling on waves of energy to reach those for whom it is intended.

We wonder about the impact of our love, our intention, on others. Does it really reach those who lie across the ocean?

Various means exist for measuring the energy we feel and the energy we send. With divining rods, also known as dousing rods, we can measure the emotional energy of a person, plant, or pet. Then we can enter the Well and have the intention of sending love to them. When we measure again afterwards, there will be a marked and noticeable difference. In a group situation, sending love to one person will expand their emotional energy many-fold.

Without divining rods, we can observe changes in behavior. This is especially powerful if the person or object on the receiving end is not well, is in conflict, or is in the midst of painful emotion. Here on the island, we decide that we will send loving thoughts at least twice a day for a week to one person, then notice what effect our thoughts and energy have had on them.

Think now about a person, pet, element of Nature, or situation that is difficult for you to send love to – perhaps where someone is ill, in conflict, or in painful emotion. It is important to choose someone whose behavior you can observe at the end of one week. Write this person or situation in your writing tablet with your **Wand**.

This week, engage in the following experience daily:

CD Tracks 3 & 4

1. *Do one of the energy exercises – either the Chalice or the Prana Exercise. Both will heighten the experience of meditation.*
2. *Then enter the Meditation with Divine Personalities, allowing yourself to feel their energy.*
3. *Before opening your eyes, visualize sending love to the situation that you have chosen.*

If you are able to do this twice a day, the effects will be more than double. At the end of one week, notice any differences in the person or the relationship. Equally as important, observe any differences in you or your feelings toward the person or situation. Note any changes in your writing tablet.

Be aware of the energy that pours out from everywhere.

Be aware of the energy that pours out from everywhere. Be aware of the waves on the wind, the vibration of rocks, and the energy in your own hands and heart. If you are so moved, share one or more of these exercises or meditations with others, for there is increased energy in a group. 'When two or more of you are gathered in my name,' there will also be Divine Presence.

7 | *The Ocean of Being*

Be still
and know that ye are God.

We stand on the beach looking out to sea. Our spirit resonates with the stillness that permeates the ocean and its depths. Yet we know that within that stillness is a rich and infinitely varied life. Fish, dolphins, crustaceans, turtles, coral, seaweeds – a vast array of life forms. It is true on land as well: The world is teeming with life, yet within that life is a Divine tranquility, a unifying and nurturing wholeness that pervades everything. We have experienced that Presence for ourselves, with our own sensory perception.

An ocean breeze wafts over us, bringing the scent of salt and the tingle of ocean spray. We allow the breeze to breathe us, to enliven our cells with its sweet, pure air.

A fine mist begins to form on the horizon. It moves toward the beach in a dewy cloud that crosses the sea and passes over us as quickly as it came. We feel it is a message meant for us, a communication from the elemental forces of the Universe, although we are not sure what it signifies.

The waves rise and fall in a rhythm that seems to echo the beating of our heart. We feel the resonance deep within. What is this resonance, and why do the waves touch us so? We consider the waves and where they come from. They are concentrated aspects of the ocean that heave in response to the planets, yet each wave knows the ocean depths as its source. They are tangible evidence of a deeper, greater force.

We are filled with gratefulness for all that has transpired. An image of the Pool forms in our thoughts, reminding us that we wish to be aware of synchronicities and acknowledge them. We recall the light that emanated from our being and find that we are still stunned by its brilliance and the possibility that what we saw is who we really are.

When we left the Pool and fell into doubt, we found ourselves trapped in the Briar of Beliefs. Yet, when we were willing to let go of the beliefs, they faded away, like a veil parting to reveal the Ever-Present. By being open to the Ever-Present on various levels, more understanding came to us.

We recall the rainbow and the feeling of peacefulness that came while we stood in the light of the meadow. Now, as we hold this image and sensation, a rainbow begins to form over the ocean. Its base is far wider than that of any rainbow we have seen before, its hues brilliant. It is an auspicious rainbow – and a synchronicity. Our thinking about a rainbow has inspired Spirit to create one for us. In fact, it is a double synchronicity, because we have just remembered to be aware of synchronicities, and immediately one presented itself to us.

We have become the catalyst of our own synchronicities.

In truth, we have become the catalyst of our own synchronicities. This is an amazing thought. Through Spirit, the physical world has responded, reminding us that the Divine is always present. As we become more aware and attuned to the Divinity in everything, the physical world increasingly mirrors our thoughts and feelings. We perceive more synchronicities, and by noticing that we are creating synchronicity, we get a glimpse that we are One with the Divine.

We take out our Wand to write down these insights. As we write, a new thought comes to us: Spirit creates experiences that allow us to acknowledge its existence, thus moving us toward greater understanding.

We have heard that we create our own reality, but we never really believed it. Certainly, there are times when we can see the effects of our thoughts and actions on the world. Now, however, we understand that our willingness to experience the Ever-Present has a powerful effect on what shows up in our lives. Likewise, when we are caught up in the past or future, that must affect what happens as well. At those times when our thoughts are taking us away from the present, we miss the synchronicities. We miss the Divine that's happening in the moment, which is where the action is.

A Chorus of Waves

Our attention shifts to the ocean and the waves once more, where Divinity spills forth in *this* moment. The waves seem to have increased in amplitude, falling onto the beach with great force. They rise up in graceful arcs before emptying themselves of their power and rolling across the sand to disappear at our feet.

'We have a story for you,' says a voice that issues from an incoming wave.

'We too have a story,' says another wave as it tumbles to shore.

Suddenly there is a chorus of voices, all baritones and altos. 'Ah, we have stories we could tell!'

We listen to the cacophony of voices as they spill over the rocks.

'Tony's story,' says one wave.

'Paul's,' says another.

'And Sarah's,' says a third.

'Stories of people who did not notice Spirit's movement in their lives,' says a fourth wave.

As we acknowledge the waves with a nod, a second rainbow begins to form, closer to us than the first. Its base dissolves into a pool of water directly in front of us. It appears that Spirit is really trying to get our attention! And it's working.

'Tony wished for an opportunity to train corporate executives,' says one wave. 'But when the phone rang from a large corporation, he did not believe they were interested in hiring him and referred the caller to a business associate. To his astonishment, the associate reaped many months of work and financial benefit. Tony did not believe the call was for him because he carried a lifelong pattern of low self-worth. As a result, he missed out on his heart's desire.' As soon as its story is told, the wave falls back into the total consciousness of the ocean.

'And Paul,' says the next wave, 'was offered a chance to record his music at a local radio station. He deferred, saying he was too busy on his carpentry job. He allowed the chance to pass him by, unaware of how his concerns about the future – fears of being a success as a musician – were affecting his life.' At this, the wave slides back to the ocean and dissolves in the coastal tides.

'Sarah was a beautiful spirit who sought God in everything,' says a wave. 'She acknowledged synchronicities where she saw them and gave thanks as often as she could. Yet she was caught in a story about her past that she was unable to shake. She felt traumatized by the events of her childhood and believed God had treated her unfairly. Inside her, these beliefs worked like a toxin, creating a serious illness.'

As this wave ebbs, another continues. 'The illness, which presented the opportunity for Sarah to release her old beliefs, only reinforced them. Now she felt that she was being treated even more unfairly. The more God tried to get her attention through critical events, the more angry she felt. There was more illness and eventually a car accident, which signaled the end of her life.'

Yet another wave picks up the story. 'Her previous missed opportunities so tainted the vessel of her body that she was unable to hold any greater understanding, and it was necessary for her to don a new vessel. She had advanced beyond her body's ability to hold her Divinity.'

A wave that began far out to sea speaks as it rolls toward shore. 'All three of these people were manifesting from the story they carried with them, and from their unconsciousness of how it was affecting their lives. Humans have the power of creation. But most of what they create pulls them away from their Divinity. Most people are creating cycles of trauma and drama.'

At this, the voices of the waves grow silent.

We recognize that, in their silence, the waves are encouraging us to look for the presence of Spirit in our own life.

Suddenly a third rainbow appears between the near rainbow and the far one, all three present at the same time. This rainbow ends at a large rock about 30 feet from shore, creating an illumined, sacred spot. Three stories, three rainbows.

The waves have subsided, and the water is shallow enough for us to wade to the rock. Honoring the message of the rainbow, we hoist our quiver and step into the salty foam, not bothering to look at the map or the keys. We know that our next experience awaits us in the Ocean of Being.

Divinity Speaks . . . Self to self

The rock that awaits us is an observation point in the ever-moving ocean. We sit down cross-legged facing the horizon and immediately are awed by the expanse of sky and sea. Above us, puffs of cumulus clouds float toward the beach, as frigate birds sail on the air currents. Water laps gently at the rock. To our right is a cove where fishes swim within the bounds of a coral reef. The water near the reef is a light, gemlike blue.

The tide is slowly rising, and small fish have begun to swim around our rock – tiny iridescent blue ones, long thin yellow ones, others striped pink and black. A single white fish, numinous as if glowing from within, weaves among the others. It circles the rock three times before coming to stillness in the water in front of us, where it raises its head and upper body, as though resting on its anterior fins.

The white fish speaks. 'I am what many religions know as the voice of the Holy Spirit or Great Spirit, yet I am no different from you. I have come to assist you in this time of transition from self to Self. You have lived your life in the realm of time. More recently, you have begun to experience the space that time sits in.'

'You mean the Ever-Present? It was a beautiful experience.'

'It *is* a beautiful experience,' says the fish.

We smile. 'The Ever-Present always is, isn't it? We just need to learn how to find it.'

'And how did you find it before?'

'By walking into the light inside the meadow.'

'And again in the Well?'

'Yes, of course!' We had forgotten that we could enter the Ever-Present any time we enter the Well.

'You have identified with your thoughts and forgotten your experience. You have also identified with your personality, or ego, which has a beginning and an end. But you can shift from seeing yourself as finite, to *being* infinite – from being a personality to the essence of everything.' The white fish has begun to swim in slow, graceful circles, creating a corona of light around its

We can enter the Ever-Present any time we enter the Well.

luminous body. 'Knowing yourself as the essence of everything is to recognize your completeness. Like a circle, you have no beginning, no end.'

'That seems like a lot to expect from a mere human!' Yet we laugh, as we are beginning to feel a bit more than merely human.

'In the Ever-Present, which is beyond time, you experienced the realm of unity with all things. This realm of unity is Being.'

'The Ever-Present and Being – is there really a difference between them?'

'Being is the quality that fills the Ever-Present.' The fish has stopped circling in order to face us again, spreading its fins wide. 'It includes the waves and the ocean, the shore, the top and the bottom of everything. The waves are an indicator of personality, the small self. Each personality may be limited in its perspective of the depths, but the ocean encompasses all of it. It is the totality of the manifested as well as the unmanifested – all levels, all dimensions.'

*You **are** that – the being that is ever-present, everywhere.*

'And we can experience ourselves as *that?*' It's an awesome thought.

'Indeed, you can. You *are* that – the being that is ever-present, everywhere. And then, nowhere!'

The sun has begun to set, and the profusion of color – orange, aqua, mauve, violet – stuns our senses. We still our mind, in order to experience this glorious beauty more fully. The colors of sky wash over and through us, continuing to change as they grow muted and subdued. The white fish waits silently by.

We have the thought that we wish to visit with the Divine personalities.

'You will visit the Divine beings,' says the fish. Like the other creatures of the Ever-Present, it knows what is in our mind – as though we and they are one being. 'I will leave now and allow other teachers to assist you.' The fish waves a fin and dives deep, merging with the water.

Closing our eyes, we enter the silence of the Well.

Conversation with Divine Personalities – *Close your eyes, breathe, and relax. Feel the breath in the body – the sensations at the tip of the nose, inside the nose and throat, in the lungs and abdomen.*

After a few moments, visualize yourself at the edge of a forest, about to enter a meadow. Before you enter, place to your left all feelings, thoughts, and concerns about the past. To the right, place all thoughts, feelings, and concerns about the future. Take a few moments to do this. Then visualize all the energy that has been tied up in the past and future returning to you. See yourself becoming lighter, your energy more vibrant.

Now step into the meadow. Before you is an arch – perhaps a rainbow – from which a golden light is glowing. You walk to the arch, step through it, and enter the light. Feel the light on your skin, on your breath, and in the cells of your body.

After a few moments, look into the light and see a figure coming toward you. As it approaches, you see it is the figure of Buddha. Allow him to come close and stand before you. Take a few moments to feel his energy. Once you can feel it, he leans forward and embraces you, honoring you as Divine. Buddha then steps aside, allowing another Divine personality to come forth.

Do this process three more times. The second personality to come forward is Mary, the mother of Jesus. Feel her energy. Then experience her embracing you and acknowledging you as Divine. The third personality is Shiva, the Hindu personality that represents the Creator. Don't judge the experience. Simply feel their energy, and allow them to honor you as Divine. A fourth Divine being steps forward. You know instinctively who this is. Feel their energy and allow them to honor you as Divine.

All four stand before you. Now, allow these four to engage with you in whatever way they wish. Be open to any messages or experiences that come. Ask any questions of them that you wish.

When all four have honored and communicated with you, they join hands and form a circle around you. Be present with their energy for 15 to 20 minutes. If your mind wanders, return to this blessed circle of Divinity.

We open our eyes, feeling deeply at peace in the Ocean of Being. Night has come, and stars fill the sky.

We feel deeply at peace in the Ocean of Being.

Our visitation with the Divine Ones was illuminating. We feel honored that they have acknowledged us as Divine. Each of them touched our head and blessed us. This has helped us go from a place of limitation – this mind, this body, this skin – to feeling incredible vastness.

We asked the Virgin Mary to tell us what it is like to be supplicated by humans asking for her assistance. Is it a drain on her energy and her love? 'No,' she answered. 'Energy and love are boundless. They are without limit.'

We asked Kuan Yin, feminine bodhisattva and goddess from Asia, to tell us about Being, what it feels like, and she answered, 'Being is peaceful, joyful, and full of bliss. It is an ever-present deep satisfaction that never fades.'

Experiences with the Divine personalities can be magical and fun. Louise, another traveler to the Isle of Is, found herself dancing with Jesus. David laughed as he described teeing off with the spiritual masters. Buddha told Mick that he could let go of his feelings of guilt about an accident in which another person was injured, but rather to feel immense love for this person in his heart.

*Take up your **Wand** and free-write about your experience.*

We lie back and look up at the stars, which glimmer at us knowingly. We feel a laugh forming inside – even the stars are talking to us! As we do, a voice speaks to us, not with sound but as a knowing inside us. It is the ocean itself, the Ocean of Being.

I am Consciousness, the voice says.

'I am Consciousness,' the voice says. 'I am beyond all realms of your beliefs. I am what shows up in all major religions. Some call me the Absolute. Others call me the Self.'

Our spirit hears and understands these words. We are like a tuning fork, and the words are vibrations that reverberate inside.

'You are that which you seek,' the voice continues. 'The truth of what you seek is already here. Not only are you living in the Ever-Present, in a state of Being, but you are that Being – verb, noun, all of it.'

'We wish for more experiences of this,' we say. 'How might we find this place when we return home?'

'You entered the Isle of Is through the Gate of Gratitude,' says the voice. 'Gratitude is the highest, quickest way to be in a state of Being. It arouses a feeling of devotion, and devotion to God is the highest path.'

We think about gratitude arousing devotion, how the purity of the feeling of gratitude flows easily into feelings of devotion. A Robert Frost poem called 'Devotion' comes to mind, one we came across years ago. We wonder if this is what Frost felt:

The heart can think of no devotion
greater than being shore to ocean,
holding the curve in one position,
counting the endless repetition.

'Devotion to God is devotion to your Self,' the voice continues. 'Remember what Jesus said, that the kingdom of God is within. To understand what it is that you really are, be devoted to your Self.'

This is a new idea, and strange to us. 'How might we do that?' we ask. There is so much we wish to take home with us, so much we wish to remember.

'Practice what you are learning here . . . gratitude, acknowledgement, exploring those beliefs that limit you from knowing yourself as Divine, visiting the Ever-Present and the Ocean of Being through meditation, and experiencing the waves of energy.'

Of course. We have experienced all that and can do so again.

'Divinity is your true identity. Allow this to be the thought that you carry through your days and into your nights.'

We wonder what it is that keeps us from experiencing it all the time. 'Forgetting' is what we told Conscious Caterpillar. But is there more? Here on the island we have fewer distractions than we will have once we return to our home town. Yes, distractions are another way we might keep from experiencing Being.

Divinity is your true identity. Carry this thought into your days and nights.

*Consider the statement, 'Divinity is my true identity.' What if this were true? With your **Wand**, write your thoughts in response. Write for 10 minutes without stopping.*

Now consider what it is that keeps you from experiencing this all the time. Write for 10 minutes more.

'Divinity is my true identity.' Write the statement on slips of paper to put in your wallet or purse and tape to your refrigerator and mirror. This will help you attune more and more to the aspects, qualities, and vibration of Divinity.

Do this for three weeks. It will change your perception.

'Several hindrances can keep you from having the experience of Being all the time,' says the Ocean. 'One of these – your beliefs – you have already explored. Further aspects of the island will help you understand and be liberated as well. Now it is time for you to go. Remember that Being knows no time or space: You are always in the Ever-Present, in the realm of Being.'

The night has passed with ease. The waves, which are the heart of the Divine pulsing out into the relative world, have again receded. It is time to re-enter the material realm, and we wade to shore.

Walking up the beach to pick up our shoes, we spot a signpost several yards to our right. As we head toward the sign, a corked bottle lodged in the sand catches our attention. While retrieving the bottle, it occurs to us that even the messages are coming from all directions.

8 | *The Forest of Forgetfulness*

Ye cannot travel far from Is-ness.
Your Divine Mother

We head for the signpost, where three signs point in different directions. They are legible from a distance. **Mount Metaphor** points straight ahead, toward a mountain slope that emerges above the rainforest. Another, **The Swamp of Illusion**, points right, to a trail that winds along the beach, then turns sharply inland. The third, **The Forest of F**, points left toward a thicket. Part of the sign is missing. We wonder what the **F** stands for. Faith? Focus? Fantasy? We take out the keys and map to see which sign to follow, but they offer no clue.

Curious about what is in the bottle, we tug on the cork and take a peek. Inside is a rolled-up sheet of blue stationery on which is scribbled a handwritten note. We unroll it carefully. It's from Mother! How did Mother know where to find us?

Dear Sweetie,
How are you? I ran into Anna in town, and she told me you had gone off to an island somewhere. I didn't quite catch the name. Those places

have spiders, so I hope you're careful. Are you having fun? We miss you.

I wanted to remind you that Grandpa is having his 89th birthday this week. He fell off a ladder yesterday and they took him to the hospital to see if he broke anything. Maybe you could send him a card. It would cheer him up. Grandma can't stay away from the bottle long enough to look at the calendar and see what day it is, so I know he'd be glad to hear from you.

Also, Jane's boyfriend walked out on her while they were at the bowling alley – she'd just had a strike, too – and she hasn't heard from him since. I never did like him much, but your sister seems to fall for these unpredictable types. She's awful upset, and you're the only person she'll talk to. Can you give her a call?

My bursitis has been acting up. Your mother's getting to be an old lady, I guess. All these troubles get me down, too. I reckon I'd feel a mite better if the sun would come out. Fluffy's not eating right, and I need to get her to the vet. Maybe you can do that when you get home. I can't pay for it till I get my retirement check. You can pick up my prescription for antacid at the same time.

Oh, almost forgot, someone broke into the La Rosas' house last night and stole their TV. I'm going to get another lock for the back door, maybe put it higher up than the other four.

Well, hurry home! Do you know when you'll be back?

Love, Mother

Head down, engrossed in the letter, we bump into the signpost and veer to the left. Worldly concerns have kicked us out of awareness of the Ocean of Being.

When we look up to see where we are, Mother's letter begins to disintegrate, the ink transforming into drops of water that dissipate in our hand. To our astonishment, the bottle crumbles, turning into grains of sand. Some grains sift through our fingers and fall to the ground; others drift away on waves of light. Mother has reached out to us energetically, perhaps only in her thoughts, yet we know that the incidents related in her letter are indeed happening back home.

We feel compassion for Mother, Grandpa and Grandma, Jane, and Fluffy.

Our heart is open from being in the Ever-Present, experiencing the Waves of Energy, and immersing ourselves in the Ocean of Being. We wish to be of help, but we don't know what we can do from here.

Dark has descended around us. The trees are tall and scraggly, seeking the sun; their branches form a tangled canopy above. Splinters of light peek through the leaves, but so little comes through that the trees and underbrush have grown scrawny and undernourished. It seems like an unhappy place. Why are we back in the forest again?

We are most concerned about our family and wish they could come to the isle themselves. A holiday would do them all good. More importantly, as we are learning, an experience of the Ever-Present might help them let go of their worries about the past and future. They might be able to find joy in the present moment.

Mother has been concerned about her health for years, and she worries about her children, wanting us to be happy and have good lives. Our shoulders tense just thinking about Mother and the burglary. Then there's Grandpa and Grandma. Thinking about their troubles makes us feel anxious. Our stomach is tight, and our brow throbs. We feel tired, our eyelids droopy, and we want to lie down, but the ground is covered with loose dirt and rocks.

Suddenly we feel worried about what we are to do here. Will some creature show up to talk to us? Perhaps our map will be of help. On the map, a trail has indeed been etched from the beach, past the signpost, and into the forest. It leads to a gnarled tree.

We glance around, looking for such a tree. Ah, yes, over there is a tree with a thick and knotty trunk, unlike the others. Its many branches curve up and down, this way and that, forming a leafy lattice. It seems to be a very old tree.

Approaching, we spy a telephone nailed to its trunk. A sign says **U-PAY**, and beside it is a note: *Long & distant calls only.* Maybe we could call Mother, Grandpa, and Jane from here. There's no place to buy a birthday card, that's for sure. When we get home, we could take Grandpa to an Al Anon meeting, so he could talk to others about Grandma's drinking. And we can offer to take Jane to have her Tarot cards read, or treat her to a facial. We can certainly buy a lock and affix it to Mother's back door.

We dig in our pockets, but we don't have cash or a credit card to pay for a phone call. Then we notice letters carved higher on the tree: **fone home**. Is this a synchronicity? Are the words carved just for us?

Suddenly the phone begins to ring. Dee-Vine-ingggg. Dee-Vine-ingggg.

Who could be calling here? We pick up the receiver. 'Hello?'

'Hello, hello,' says a woman's voice echoing from eternity. 'This is your Divine Mother.'

A woman's voice echoes from eternity: This is your Divine Mother.

Is . . . Is . . . Is . . . Is

'Divine Mother?' We are puzzled.

'Yes,' says the voice. 'Your biological mother is a lovely lady. She's a reflection of me, but I am the infinite Divine Mother. We are at your service. You see, you can never travel far from Is-ness.'

These last words seem familiar, as though we have recently heard or seen them.

'You are concerned about your mother,' she says, 'as well as others in your family.'

'Yes! We just got a letter from Mother. She wants us to come home and help her.'

'And what feelings does this bring up in you?' Her voice exudes love and interest in us.

'We feel helpless because we can't be there. But then, we often feel helpless around their problems. There's only so much we can do.'

'Yet you wish to help,' she says. 'To help, to help' echoes after.

'Yes.' We think for a moment. 'We also want to feel at peace. It's hard for us to do that when we get caught up in their lives.' It's also hard to believe that just an hour ago we were immersed in the Ocean of Being!

'These distresses are about others, but ultimately they are about yourself. You identify with others' difficulties. You enter the drama, by allowing their situation to spark your own fears, doubts, and feelings about mortality.'

It is true. We have lost our sense of peace and joy, now replaced by physical discomfort and memories of our own past . . . a sweetheart leaving us . . . an alcoholic co-worker who committed suicide . . . being in physical danger.

'Divine Mother, where are we? Our map doesn't tell us what this place is. We wish to know.'

'Ah! It is the Forest of Forgetfulness,' she says tenderly. 'You have become caught up in everyone else's problems and identified them as your own. You have also sought answers outside yourself, forgetting to acknowledge your Divine self and the wisdom within. You have forgotten to enter the Well.'

'Oh,' we say, realizing this is true. It's as though we had never experienced the Ocean of Being – yet the memory of Being resides inside us, too. As we think about Being, a wave of peacefulness washes through us.

As we observe what has happened since reading Mother's letter, we see that our thoughts, emotions, and body sensations changed markedly as a result. 'Memories of the past can have a powerful effect, can't they?'

'Indeed, old memories make their home in the body's cells,' she says. 'When memories are stimulated by current events – and by our thoughts about the events – fear, doubt, and anxiety take over. These fears and doubts are not from the Ever-Present. Like the memories, they are from the past. Yet we bring them into our present.'

'We just came from the Ocean of Being!' we exclaim. 'How can it be that we would forget and turn away so quickly?'

How can it be that we would turn away so quickly?

'Your culture, and the society in which you live, do not understand that feelings are clues for where healing is needed. They do not teach you that if you are present with the feelings, not pushing them away, they will dissolve. Instead, your culture provides many distractions to prevent you from feeling fully in the present. What is not understood is that the feelings do not go away of their own accord. By distracting one's self from the feelings, they are pushed down, only to resurface at a later time.

'Outwardly seeking happiness and pleasure never brings lasting fulfillment. The Ocean of Being can be found everywhere, in everything. But amidst all the world's distractions, it may be more difficult to remember. Visiting the Well allows you to easily find the being that you already are.'

'What distractions, Divine Mother? Like alcohol and drugs?'

'Those are easy to recognize because the damage they do is so visible. Yet there are many more – tobacco; excessive quantities of food and habits of eating at all hours; sex; television; movies; computer games; sports; work; relationships – any place where a person engages compulsively, shall we say, without complete freedom in their thoughts and feelings.'

We nod, remembering the letter. 'We recognize our self in that list.'

'And what distractions do *you* use when your feelings come to the surface, in an attempt to not feel them?'

'Television. Food, for sure. Maybe more.'

'Perhaps you will write about this?'

We switch the phone to the other ear, so as to take out our Wand.

'Let the phone hang for a few minutes,' she says. 'I'll wait while you pen your thoughts. After all, I'm aware of my infinite Presence. Time is of no concern for me.'

With your **Wand** *and writing tablet, use free writing to answer these questions: 'What distractions do I use when I don't wish to feel my feelings. And what feelings am I hoping not to feel?' Take enough time to answer these questions, perhaps 10-15 minutes, to allow your thoughts and feelings to surface as you write. Continue to ask: 'What additional distractions do I use? What additional feelings would I like to not feel?'*

When we have finished writing, we clasp the phone again. 'Divine Mother? We learned that we try to distract ourselves when we feel lonely or bored. And we use many distractions: sugary foods, beer, TV, computer games, movies. But the toughest one to look at is that we try to use relationships to make ourselves feel better. And not so successfully, either.'

'It's an important observation: Distracting is only successful in the moment, not in the long run.'

We make a note of this in our writing tablet as a reminder for the days ahead.

'You have searched your soul honestly,' she says. 'Let us look at the lonely and the bored. Humans only feel these things when they forget who they are. Is Divinity lonely? Is Divinity bored? What do you think?'

Is Divinity lonely?
Is Divinity bored?

We laugh. 'We think that Spirit is not lonely. The Universe is not bored.'

'Exactly so. That's the way it is . . . is . . . is . . . is.'

The reverberation of Is-ness hangs in the air.

A Heavenly Hand

'Dear one,' says Divine Mother, 'what about your mother's letter? What feelings does it bring up in you?'

'There are many. We remember our first love, who left us standing at the altar. We thought we would die from the pain. And grief for Grandma and our friend Luke, who both drink too much. It's hard to see them hurting themselves. And the physical danger.' We stop talking because memories of physical danger have begun to course through us, one after the other, in rapid succession. We are beginning to feel overwhelmed.

Divine Mother knows what we are experiencing. 'Wish you to tell me one of these memories?'

'A tough one?' we ask, unsure if we should call the painful memories into even greater focus.

'Yes, the toughest one,' she says. 'When you are willing to enter the most difficult pain of the past, the easier ones will fall by the wayside too.'

We take a deep breath. 'There are two. First, when we were 11 years old, we were hit by a car. We spent six months in the hospital, and the doctors weren't sure we would live.'

'And you were just a child. This helps explain your mother's fears for her children, doesn't it?' says Divine Mother. 'And the other?'

'We were robbed, beaten, and left for dead when we were 21. The robber threatened to slash our throat.' Telling the stories has activated our body's memory. We have begun to shake from head to foot.

'Ah, the old fear,' Divine Mother says tenderly. 'You are feeling it now. Shaking is your body's way of releasing it. But perhaps additional understanding will also help.'

Still shaking, we see that more light is entering the forest. A ray of sunlight is streaming down, creating a yellow carpet in front of the tree.

'Put on these glasses,' she says. 'See how Divine Presence has kept you alive. See how it has placed a heavenly hand on the one who threatened you, like a guardian angel.'

See how Divine Presence has kept you alive.

A kingfisher, royal blue and white, sweeps down and drops a pair of lavender-tinted glasses at our feet. We pick them up and put them on. Around us, the forest recedes from focus, as the scene of the car accident begins to play. We are on our bicycle, and a speeding car slams on its brakes. We hear the crash and feel ourselves dashed to the pavement.

Then a Presence enters the scene of the accident, lifting us from the pavement and cradling us until the ambulance arrives. When we are placed in the ambulance, this Presence stays at our side. It goes with us to the hospital, wrapping itself around us in the emergency room and when we go in for surgery. We are awed watching the scene.

This fades, and a dark alleyway comes forth – the scene of the robbery. We walk down the street, hands in our pockets, our thoughts on having just lost our job. We are unaware that we are being followed. Suddenly we are thrust into the alley, knocked to the ground, and pummeled with fists. The assailant holds a knife to our throat. But a Presence comes forth and restrains the knife a few inches from our throat. We are surrounded by a field of energy, visible with the glasses, which protects us from further danger.

'This is the intercession in your world that you don't normally see,' says Divine Mother. 'In the moment that you might have been physically harmed, the angelic presence intervened.'

'We are astonished to see this, and deeply moved. We had no idea.'

'What is good to notice is that the robber changed. He intended to kill you, and then he backed away because he became aware that you were protected. He could not articulate this, but he had a knowing that you would be safe and that he could not harm you. Divine Presence transformed him enough to prevent him from killing you or harming you further. He quite literally had a change of heart. Does this help you to see things in a different light?'

'So we weren't alone.' Tears come to our eyes.

'Indeed not,' says the Mother. 'This, too, is synchronicity. Divine intervention – Spirit – God – Being – came to your aid.'

We wonder if it could be true. And yet our heart seems to know this is the case.

'It is marvelous that you are recognizing these things now. It will help you when you receive further instructions on how to deal with your feelings in a constructive manner.'

'Thank you so much, Divine Mother. We are most grateful for your assistance.'

'It is an honor for me to be with you,' she says. 'This time of speaking on the phone has come to an end, but you can always call me. Simply utter my name. For now, take out your Wand and reflect on what we have said here.'

There's a loud click, and a dial tone.

Gently we place the phone back on its nail, take out our Wand and writing tablet, and sit in the sunshine that is spilling onto the forest floor.

*With **Wand** in hand, consider these questions: What in my life pulls me away from Spirit/God/Presence? What fears? Desires? Old memories and old pain? For at least 10 minutes, list your answers to each of these four things – fears, desires, old memories, and old pain.*

Now pick one of the most difficult things to have happened in your life. Write down what the situation was, how it felt then, and how it feels now. How is it affecting your life?

When you have finished writing, visualize Divine Presence intervening in the situation. See it with the eyes of Divinity.

'Be present with the feelings this brings up.' It is the voice of Divine Mother. We look around, but she is nowhere visible. 'By being present and not turning away from the feelings, they will transmute and be released into another realm. When you allow yourself to be focused on the sensations of the physical body, you open up a portal for Divine Presence to enter and remove the blocks that are holding the feelings in. The light dispels the darkness of what is being held there. The light that now enters the forest will also enter you.'

We sit quietly. What do we feel? And where in our body do we feel it?

*****Presence Practice** – Enter now a state of Presence using this simple five-part technique: Breathe. Relax. Feel. Observe. Love. Take a few moments with each part.*

CD Track 5:

Presence Practice

*****Breathe.** Bring your awareness to your breath. Deepen your breath.*

*****Relax.** Breathe and relax deeply into the breath, into the body.*

*****Feel.** Feel what is happening in your body. Feel the sensations. Feel the breath, the inhalation, the expansion of lungs and abdomen, and the exhalation. Feel all the sensations of the body without judgment.*

*****Observe.** Observe the sensations. Allow the light of the Ever-Present to shine on the sensations. Merely observe them.*

*****Love.** Embrace the feelings, the sensations, and the body with your own Divine love, as though they are your child or loved one.*

Continue this process, repeating the steps, for at least 10 minutes.

e can consciously invite in Divine Presence.

When thoughts of past experiences surface in the present – or when we recognize their effect on us in the present – we can consciously invite in Divine Presence. By taking the opportunity to observe memories and sensations in the way just described, they begin to dissipate. The sensations and fears, which reside in the darkness, lose their grip when we shine the light of Divinity on them. We may not yet recognize ourselves as Divine, but we can muster the Presence of God or Spirit to come in.

When we are aware – observing and feeling – the Forest ceases to be Forgetting, and we are returned easily and gently to the Ever-Present. Conscious Caterpillar told us that what we think of as miraculous becomes commonplace. These miracles show up as Divine intervention protecting us. Often, when we are saved from danger, we think 'we were lucky that time.' Yet the Self is indeed looked after, taken care of, nourished, honored, and loved.

By visiting the Ocean of Being through meditation, we open up Divine Presence and Divine intervention to be even more present in our daily experience. That's what allowed the phone to ring, with Divine Mother on the other end.

The Many E. Satvas

The sun has begun to shine brightly in this aspect of the forest; the tree trunks have grown thicker, their branches more lush. Green is everywhere, pulsing and vibrant. Even the air is fresher. We stand and take a deep breath, stretching our arms overhead. Ah! That's better.

Our eyes fall on a small clearing just a few feet away. There is something on the grass, striped red and white. Upon closer examination, we see that it is a ring of mushrooms, like tiny circus tents. We walk closer and stoop to look. On each mushroom sits a fairy with gauzy wings.

'Who are you?' we ask in our mind.

'Why, fairies, of course!' says one, standing up. 'Mother Divine sent us.'

'It's your mothers who have sent ye to talk with us,' says another. The voice coming from a fairy in the back is oddly familiar. This fairy wears a captain's hat.

'Ferryman?' we ask in disbelief.

'Aye.' He grins and bows. 'This ring of mushrooms, in ancient lore, was associated with fairies, and with fairies honoring unfoldment and new beginnings.' He leans toward us as though to share a secret. 'Actually, there is never a beginning – or an ending. It just appears that way to the one looking on. For the one walking through the door, it is a continuance. We fairies,' he winks at the others, 'honor continuance.'

The fairies sway on their mushrooms moving their hands back and forth in a gospel kind of rhythm. 'Con-tin-u-ance,' they sing, swaying their hips.

'We have a story to tell ye.' He motions for us to sit. 'Ye may have heard this story before, but that's quite alright. The best stories can be told over and over forever.'

The other fairies clap their tiny hands in anticipation.

'It's the story of a flood. Ye remember Noah and the Ark?'

We nod. 'Of course.'

'Well, this is a different flood, but it too is about Divine communication and those willing to listen. In this story a farmer named Benjamin was caught at home when the floodwaters came, so he climbed up on his roof. He got mighty worried watching animals and pieces of furniture float by as the waters continued to rise, and he prayed to God to save him.

'While he's sitting there, a neighbor comes by rowing his dinghy, the Boat E. Satva. *Get in!* yells the neighbor. Benjamin yells back, *Thanks! But I'm waiting for God to save me!* And the neighbor floats away.'

'Oh, no!' cry the fairies. 'What is Benjamin thinking?'

'In a little while, a cow comes by real close to Ben's roof. Ben thinks, well, I could get on the cow, but I better wait for God. The cow is so close that Ben sees a tag around its neck. It's the cow Esatva.'

'Yay, yay!' call the fairies. 'It's the cow Esatva.'

'Now, sure enough, it's a modern-day tale, and a heli-satva-copter spots Ben on the roof. It hovers real close and sends down a rope. *Hop on!* calls the pilot. *I'll take ye to dry land!* But Ben does what?'

The fairies all stand and wave their hands. 'He stays on the roof!'

'So, of course, Benjamin dies in the flood. But that's not the end of the story, being that we all live after. He goes up to the pearly gates and asks Saint Peter to be let into Heaven. Peter checks his roster. *Why are ye here?* he asks Ben. *Ye aren't supposed to be here.*

'*Well,* says Ben, *I was waiting for God to save me.*

Actually, there is never a beginning – or an ending.

'But, Benjamin, ye took away our options. God sent a boat and a cow and a copter, and ye ignored all three.'

The Fairy Man takes a second bow, and the fairies flutter up and down on their mushrooms, dancing all around.

'That's a good story,' we say. 'It's about recognizing Divine Presence where it shows up.'

'Aye,' he nods. 'And it shows up everywhere.'

*Take up your **Wand** and ask yourself: 'What is it that pulls **me** away? What is it that seems so much more important than recognizing Divinity in everything? In recognizing that Divinity is the essence of my Self?'*

Write for 15 minutes without stopping. If you run out of thoughts, ask yourself the questions again, and write down the answers that come. Allow the same thoughts or new thoughts to come to you. Dig deeper. The deeper you are willing to go, the more helpful will be the process of writing. By uncovering what has been hidden, we bring things into the light, where they dissolve and drift away.

When we have written, we find ourselves wishing to be in silence and desiring to connect with the Divine personalities.

The Fairy Man nods at us, understanding. 'Aye, 'tis good for ye,' he says. We close our eyes.

Meditation with Divine Personalities – the basic steps
- *Set down the past.*
- *Set down the future.*
- *Step into the Light.*
- *Invite the Divine personalities forward.*
- *Allow each one to acknowledge you as Divine.*
- *Remain in silence for a total of 20-30 minutes.*

Do this meditation twice a day, as a regular practice, from now on.

We feel both enlivened and at peace after this meditation and look around for the fairies, but they have vanished – all except the Fairy Man himself, who sits on the one remaining mushroom.

'How'd it go?' he asks, smiling.

'Great! We feel reconnected to the Divine in everything.'

'And do ye even feel Divine ye-self?' he asks, winking.

'We're beginning to.' We laugh.

'Good, then. Well, I'll be off. And ye'll be off, too, to Mount Metaphor, where ye'll take a fresh look at your images and beliefs. And ye'll have the fun of remembering.' He waves and disappears quicker than a flash.

We wonder, shouldering our quiver, what a metaphor has to do with remembering.

9 | *Mount Metaphor*

Ye live by metaphor,
and that is the truth.

The Book of Life

We emerge from the Forest of Forgetfulness, grateful for the reminder that our fears, and our tendency to distract ourselves from these fears, have kept us from living in the Ever-Present immersed in the Ocean of Being. Fear and the folly of distraction have put us to sleep, like the poppy fields in the Wizard of Oz. How easily such a lapse in consciousness allows us to forget who we are! The Forest has assured us that it is not entirely our fault that we have forgotten; we have been conditioned to forget by the culture in which we live.

Like the other places we've visited on the Isle of Is, the Forest has nurtured us and guided us toward a deeper understanding of who we are. We wonder, though, with such wonderful support from Nature, what could possibly keep us bound to a cycle of forgetting?

Ahead stands a magnificent mountain – Mount Metaphor – its grand peak rising from the mists. Will the mountain provide answers to our question? The path that lies before us has grown thick with grass, yet traces of pixie dust make us think that it was once traversed by wizards, mystics, and fairies of old. From the bottom it appears to be a treacherous trip, yet we find that each step is easy. The rocks, the soil, the grasses lift us up as we go. It is an effortless climb to the top.

At the peak, we gaze out over the landscape of our life. The view is worth the climb: Looking out across the island, we see mist rising from the Ocean of Being. In the mist we see the reflections of our past – our far-reaching beliefs, and images upon which our beliefs are based.

The wind ripples the treetops of the Forest below. As we watch, it turns toward us and rushes up the mountain slope, calling our name. 'Come, rest, sweet one,' it seems to say. 'What you search for is here.'

We glance around for a place to sit. At our feet is a boulder we had not noticed, which is carved with an ancient inscription. The glyphs are puzzling. Yet the words 'Look Here' leap to our mind. We examine the boulder, feeling the glyphs with our fingertips, and the smooth stone upon which they are carved. We find a cache underneath. Reaching into the cache, we pull out a package wrapped in a piece of velvet.

At the peak, we gaze out over the landscape of our life.

The Book of Life

Carefully we unwrap the cloth. Inside is a book made of parchment leaves, on top of which lies a single folded sheet. We open the sheet, which is inscribed with the same strange characters we found on the rock. As we study it, a message forms itself inside our thoughts:

'Welcome, traveler! It is of great significance that you have come this far. Lean against this rock and explore in this parchment book the knowledge that will answer your deepest questions.'

A shiver of knowing moves through us. We acknowledge the synchronicity. We have just asked for assistance, and here it is, an answer to our deepest questions.

'You have visited the Gate of Gratitude,' the message continues, *'and learned that gratefulness is not something with which to respond to a specific event or object in the material world. It comes from beyond the world, a state of Being that allows you to be grateful for everything that comes your way – even the loss, the despair, and the disillusionment that may visit you from time to time.*

'You have peered into the Pool of Ac(Knowledge) and discovered how taking notice and honoring Nature's support on a daily basis brings a deepening sense of

peace. You have considered your own Briar of Beliefs and entered the realm of the Ever-Present through the gift of meditation. The Waves of Energy, the Ocean of Being, the Forest of Forgetfulness – all have brought you closer to your own true nature.

'Yet there is one thing, more than any other, that will keep you from being who you are. It is a simple thing – an image that you have taken deep inside you – an image for what you believe Life is all about.'

The message ends here.

Most curious, we open the book to the first page, where there is an odd handprint with three crooked fingers and a palm much larger than our own. We feel drawn to place our hand on top of the print, and as we do, the hand-print becomes smaller, transforming so that it matches ours exactly. 'Oh!' There is a thrill of recognition and a sense that the entire book will be spoken to us. We close our eyes.

Indeed, the book begins to speak in a soft and melodic tone:

The Book of Life

or

*How You Have Lost Your Connection
to the Essence of Life*

Dear Beloved One, This book is for you. It has waited for you, knowing that the time would come when you were ready to receive its Truth.

You are about to receive a gift of wisdom that, before you, only sages of old have been prepared to receive. Your willingness to explore the Isle of Is, to take its knowing into your Self, and to climb Mount Metaphor has readied you to receive this gift. It is for those who have arrived at an understanding of what Is, and of how they forgot.

You have always been Divine, and will always be Divine.

This is the Book of Life, and its message to you is this: *You are Divine. You have always been Divine, and you will always be Divine. You are meant to live in this place of Is as an expression of that Divinity.*

When you arrived on Earth, you were handed misconceptions and erroneous beliefs that you have unconsciously taken as truth. It is likely that your parents and your society did not experience the information that is in this book. Do not blame them for failing to point you here.

Indeed, until now, your metaphors have kept you from being ready to receive it. It is as though you were given a ticket to a theater, then when you entered the theater, you got caught up in the story, identified with one of the characters, and forgot who you really were.

The wisdom contained herein relates to the nature of the human mind and human thought. Much of what you have learned before about the mind will be of little use. We invite you to receive this wisdom with an open heart.

The reality is that the mind is an embodied object. Thought is formed in the body and in the space around you, not solely inside your brain. Your mind, body, and emotions are one whole, not elements that operate separately from each other. The mind uses metaphors, which are based in your sensory experience of sight, hearing, smell, taste, and touch, to help you make 'sense' of the world.

A metaphor, as you may recall from your school learning, is a turn of speech used to describe one thing in terms of another. Your own language contains many examples: 'The night sky is a blanket of stars.' 'Time is money.' 'Their marriage is a house of cards.' In reality, of course, the sky is not a blanket, time is not money, and marriage is not a flimsy structure made of cards. Metaphors help us grasp an idea or describe our experience by comparing it to something else.

A metaphor is much more than a figure of speech, for you think and experience your life in terms of metaphors, using your senses. You understand 'blanket of stars' because you know what a blanket looks like. You understand 'house of cards' because you have built one before, using senses of sight and touch. Money is an object in the physical world that you have counted and touched and exchanged for food and clothing. Everyone in your earthly realm uses metaphors to help them understand the material world through their senses. They also use metaphors to help them understand concepts such as 'time' and 'marriage.'

Your concepts are at the center of your understanding of the world. They structure what you perceive, how you get around in the world, and how you relate to other people.

What we wish most for you to know, dear one, is that all of

your concepts are based in metaphors. Your mind has created these associations – or adapted them from other people or from society – so that you can understand concepts *through the sensory organs of the body.* This includes your ideas about time, life, the mind, morality, affection, love, death, and much much more.

Placing the parchment book on the boulder, we stand up and look around. The mists have receded, and the island shimmers in the sunlight. To the north, we see the Pool of (Ac)Knowledge and the Forest of Forgetfulness, where we have already gained much wisdom. To the west, a path leads down the mountain slope, curving around a cave-like entrance. The dark cavity pulses with energy, a heart inside the mountain. We remember that Native Americans believe that caves are places for new awareness. Turning south, we see an idyllic landscape, so delicate and ethereal that it appears to be a transcendental dream.

What metaphors do you hold about life, love, and death?

A thought comes to us: These are metaphors, too – the landscape, a transcendental dream; and the cave, a heart in the mountain. They are metaphors for aspects of the physical world. But what about concepts? What metaphors do we hold about life, love, and death?

Eagerly we sit down again, take the book in our lap, and place our hand over the handprint.

The book begins to speak:

Of particular importance to those of you who wish to end the cycle of forgetfulness are metaphors about life itself. You see, every person, without exception, has a primary metaphor for what life is. Many people have more than one metaphor, acquired at different stages of their life – as a child, adolescent, young adult, and so on. But usually there is one metaphor that operates most powerfully in a person's life.

This metaphor we call the 'controlling life metaphor' because it sets limits on how the person lives, and because it usually does so unknown to the one whose life it runs. In general, controlling life metaphors are hidden from one's view. Often they are adopted early in life as a way to make sense of one's experience.

Let us give you some examples:

Life is a Struggle. This metaphor usually comes into a person's life when their parents are struggling to earn a living and provide food for their family. The child learns that struggling is better than the alternative, which is to give up and starve. It is a way of 'doing' in the world that involves hard work and wrestling with the enemy, in this case, poverty or unappreciative employers. The child may very well carry this metaphor into adulthood. Unlike their parents, they may earn enough to live on and feed themselves, but now the struggle is for fame or greater fortune. The metaphor permeates everything within their life – even their choice of religion, which they may hold most sacred. As long as the metaphor predominates, it is impossible for this person to experience life as anything but a struggle. The struggle continues.

Life is a Job, or a Responsibility. This may be the controlling life metaphor for someone who makes a list each morning of things to do, then spends their day working to check items off the list. Though the person may go on vacations, relaxation is brief or nonexistent. There is always more to do, more to accomplish. When they were young, their parents may have given them many responsibilities when they wished to be outside playing. A parent or other adult may have modeled the metaphor for them.

Life is a Ladder may be the metaphor for someone whose life is driven by a desire to achieve more and obtain more. This person may work in a corporate environment, climbing the ladder of artificial success. Feelings of self-worth are often tied to the metaphor, as there is always another rung to climb. If the person finds himself on a lower rung, he may feel that his life (and that he) is of lesser or no value. Inside this metaphor, everything is compared to everything else – a constant state of judging.

Life is a Journey is a common metaphor of your time. It is an improvement over the metaphors listed above because it does not imply suffering, working hard all the time, or constantly judging. Still, it involves seeking and doing and never reaching the destination. And for many people with this metaphor, the journey may be all uphill.

Life is a Search is a similar metaphor, especially among those who have become aware that it is possible to leave behind struggle and unrelenting effort. The person sees that searching may lead to a better life, as indeed it may. However, he or she may go from psychic to psychotherapist, from doctor to diviner, from workshop to wellness conference, always seeking what will make them feel whole. They look for wholeness outside of themselves. Living in this metaphor, they are stuck in a cycle of searching and can never truly find what they seek.

These are but a few of the vast number of metaphors that human beings have adopted and taken within themselves. Many controlling life metaphors are more specific than the above examples, and some are very creative. *Life is an Orphanage . . . a Jail Cell . . . a Rainy Day . . . a Shakespearean Tragedy . . . a Walk down Sesame Street.* Controlling life metaphors are often as unique as the human being who has claimed them for their own.

Such metaphors control you by limiting your life experience to the metaphor itself. *Life is a Struggle* means always struggling, no matter how many gifts the Universe gives you. *Life is a Search* means always searching, even when what you find has the potential of bringing you peace and joy. Soon even this discovery is left behind so that the search may continue. The metaphor requires that lasting peace and joy are never found.

A glorious life is your birthright.

A glorious life is your birthright. What is necessary is for you to uncover your controlling life metaphor and come to understand how it has caught you in its web. Once you have gained this understanding, it is possible for you to step out of the old metaphor and choose a new one – a metaphor that allows you to acknowledge your Divinity in every moment.

The opportunity to take these steps awaits you at the Mine in the Mountain, where you will mine for your current metaphor, and at the Vein of God, where magnificent metaphors spill from the walls like diamonds.

Several travelers have come this way and been offered the gift that this mountain offers but have been unable to move beyond their metaphor. They have cast aside this wisdom, leaving the Isle of Is to go searching for something else.

Yet, we promise you, there is no need for further search. Beloved One, there is nowhere to go. You are everything you search for.

Beloved One, you are everything you search for.

The voice stops here. There is a sudden change in the wind, and the leaves of parchment flutter back to the beginning, closing the book.

Yet we feel there is something more we wish to do: Ah, yes, open our own tablet and make some notes.

To our astonishment, inside our tablet are instructions we have never seen before, beginning with a question, *What would life be like for the person living inside each of these metaphors?* and followed by a list:

Life is an Orphanage
Life is a Jail Cell
Life is a Rainy Day
Life is a Shakespearean Tragedy
Life is a Walk down Sesame Street
Life is a House of Horrors
Life is a Rollercoaster

*Take some time to think about each of these metaphors. With your **Wand** make notes of all the ways you can think of that the metaphor might affect a person's life. Go beyond your initial thoughts, noting both positive and negative effects. This step is very important in preparing you to identify your own controlling life metaphor when you enter the Mine in the Mountain.*

We finish writing and set our Wand and tablet aside. Fascinated by the information about metaphors, we are eager to discover our own life metaphor and see how it has affected our life.

The wind stirs the trees far below. We hear the piping of birds – and voices in the distance. We listen intently and realize that we hear singing.

Mine in the Mountain

The singing seems to be coming from the trail that leads down to the cave. We walk over to the trailhead and look down. The gnomes! We haven't seen them since the Pool of (Ac)Knowledge.

With great care, we wrap the parchment book in its velvet sheath and tuck it under the rock. As we do so, the glyphs on the rock transmute into words we can read: **Follow the drinking gourd**. We recognize the phrase. It is an allusion to the Big Dipper in the night sky of the northern hemisphere, and the trail that plantation slaves followed at night to freedom. A metaphor of drinking gourd and water dipper. Will a new metaphor lead *us* to freedom?

We pack away Wand and tablet and, out of curiosity, unfold the map. The trail to Mount Metaphor rises to a peak, where a rock and a book are shown, then loops down to a cave inside the mountain. Hoisting our quiver, we start down the trail.

The gnomes are too far ahead for them to hear us if we call out, but their red hats are easy to follow. As we gain some distance on them, we make out a few of the words they are singing: 'Don't worry, mate . . . be happy.' We are walking faster now, wishing to catch up with them. Suddenly they make a sharp turn, leaving the trail and disappearing into the cave.

The dust is just settling at the cave's entrance when we arrive. Cool air emanates from the opening, wafting over us. We feel the auspiciousness of this place, a hushed silence, as though it were a cathedral. A sign is posted nearby: **The Treasure Lies Within**.

'Hello-o-o-o! Anybody there?'

Silence.

We call again. 'Hello-o-o-o!'

A gnome in red paisley shirt and brown knickers appears in the entrance, bowing low and sweeping his arm. 'Come, come,' he says, smiling. 'Keep close. Don't get lost.'

We stoop to follow him as he ambles through a low-ceilinged, winding passageway. Straw torches light the dark walls, which appear to be veined with ore. After turning and twisting a bit, the passage opens into a small brightly lit cavern, where a rough-hewn table is set for four. A pot sits on the table under a tea cozy; miniature cups wait in their saucers.

'Join us for tea?' asks a gnome in plaid shirt and knickers, while placing a tiny spoon on each saucer.

'Yes, thank you!' We lean our quiver against the cave wall, under curvy hooks upon which hang the gnomes' red hats. We glance around. A pot-bellied stove squats adjacent to one wall; three small beds line another. The coverlets are plaid, paisley, and flowered. Above the beds are pictures of female gnomes wearing dresses that match the bedspreads, all with beatific smiles.

'Ah! Our Divine Mothers,' says the third gnome, in a yellow hibiscus shirt and blue forget-me-not knickers. 'Ye have met the Divine Mother, haven't ye?'

'Indeed, we have.' We gesture toward the table, impressed that the tea is already steaming in its pot. 'You knew we were coming.'

'We know many things,' says the plaid gnome, a glint in his eye. 'Have yer-self a seat.' He pulls out a rickety chair for us, next to the table.

'So ye have made it thus far. 'Tis very good,' says the flowered gnome, plopping himself onto a three-legged stool. 'And ye wish to find yer metaphor?'

'Oh, yes. We're quite eager.' We sip the tea, which is peppermint sweetened with honey. Nearby is an odd collection of items on a wood stand, from which brightly colored flowers grow in profusion. The items remind us of our grandmother's knick-knacks. One is a ceramic fox; another is a yellow plastic watering can; still another is a miniature car garage. We make a mental note to ask later about the flowers – how they can grow inside a cave.

'Are ye ready to answer some questions?' asks the paisley gnome, pouring a heap of honey into his cup.

We nod.

'Then get out yer wand.' He gestures toward our quiver.

We bring the quiver to the table and unfasten the latch. They peer into its contents with feigned curiosity.

'A map. Some keys. A wand. And these!' Paisley gnome reaches in with a knobby hand and pulls out a pair of metal tongs and a water dipper.

'Where…? How…?' We laugh. 'They weren't there before.'

'On the Isle of Is, ye have whatever ye need,' says Plaid gnome, twisting the tip of his beard. 'There is a font inside the cave, where ye will go dipping for a new metaphor. These will come in mighty handy.'

On the Isle of Is, ye have whatever ye need.

'But first ye must find the old metaphor, the one to which ye have been a slave,' says Flowered gnome. 'We call it mining for metaphors. We ask questions, and ye write.'

'We're ready.' Our wand is in hand, tablet on the table. We're excited about doing this, hoping not to return to a state of forgetfulness.

'First question,' says Plaid gnome. 'What is life like on a good day? Use metaphors if ye can – life is a bowl of cherries, life is a sunny day, life is a walk around the block – ye get the idea? Write 10 answers to the question. Take all the time ye need.'

They slurp their tea joyously, their pinky fingers curved just so, while we write the 10 answers. It's no small challenge to stay focused on the task, with three gnomes chuckling and watching us intently. Nevertheless, the answers come easily.

'Okay, we've done that.'

'Second question,' says Paisley gnome, squinting to read our answers upsidedown. 'What is life like on a bad day? A really bad day. No holding back. Use metaphors again – life is a rainy day, a traffic jam, a house of horrors, a prison camp. Please write 10 answers to the question.'

Again they slurp noisily as we write, froth collecting on their whiskers.

*With your **Wand**, answer the question, 'What is life like on a good day?' Look for the images you hold inside you, using metaphors, not just descriptive words such as 'life is beautiful, life is pleasant.' 'Beautiful' and 'pleasant' are adjectives that do not have images or pictures to go with them. Write 10 answers to the question, taking as much time as you need.*

When you have finished, answer the question, 'What is life like on a bad day?' Again, use metaphors. Write 10 answers to the question.

By digging for the worst feeling, the really bad-day feeling, you will uncover what is keeping you from living in the Ever-Present, established in the Ocean of Being. Do not be afraid to write down graphic or horrific metaphors if they suit your feelings on a bad day. Go as deep as you can. The idea is to expose these images to the light. Again, take as much time as you need.

When you have finished writing both sets of answers, reread your lists to yourself. Do you see a pattern, especially in the second list, perhaps images that are similar in some way? On the second list, choose one or two of the images that seem to resonate especially strongly for you. Circle or star them.

'Now we're getting to the fun part!' Flowered gnome claps his hands.

'The next question is: What songs, stories, fairytales, or movies did ye love as a child? Ye know – which ones drew ye to them? Maybe ones ye sang or read or watched over and over.'

'But first,' says Plaid gnome, 'we wish to show ye some photos of earlier travelers and tell ye what they found, sitting around this very table.' He reaches under the table and pulls out a thick album with photos and slips of paper sticking out all around.

'Scoot yer chair over here,' says Paisley, blowing ore dust off the album, 'so ye can see.'

'Ah, yes, this one . . .' says Plaid. 'This is Leon, who loved *The Wizard of Oz* as a child. Read all the books and watched the movie a dozen times. See his face? Looks a little like the lion, doesn't he?'

Indeed, Leon has a yellow furry face and whiskers. We laugh!

'People do a good job of collecting their metaphors,' says Paisley. 'Leon's metaphor turned out to be *Life is a Search,* just like Dorothy, who from the beginning had the ruby slippers to take her home.'

Flowered gnome nods his head vigorously. 'In his life, it showed up as looking everywhere for answers to make himself feel whole, when everything he needed was inside him all along.'

'Here's an interesting one.' Plaid gnome has been flipping the pages, with photos and notes flying all about. 'Helen was a sweet young woman with a tragic childhood. She remembered two fairytales that she identified with as a child.'

'The Little Match Girl,' says Flowered, shaking his head. 'Such a sad story, in the cold of winter.' He shivers. 'The little girl sells matches in her bare feet as the snow falls down around her. She looks into a house and sees a Christmas feast spread on the table and a candle-lit tree with presents.'

Paisley continues. 'In the version Helen heard as a child, the mother of the house sees the match girl looking in the window, brings her inside, feeds her, and tucks her into a warm bed. But in the original version by Hans Christian Andersen, the girl dies of cold and joins her grandmother in Heaven.'

We recognize the original version. 'Oh, yes, our mother read it to us when we were young. It's very sad. We didn't like that ending. And what was the other fairytale?'

'The Ugly Duckling,' says Flowered, wringing his hands. 'Similar story, but it's about ducks. Everyone rejects the duckling – the goose mother who sat on the egg thinking it was her baby, then the farmer and the other animals. The duck freezes to the pond in winter, all alone.'

'A happy ending, that one,' says Paisley. 'In spring a flock of swans lands on his pond. He glances down and sees in the water's reflection that he has become a swan himself!' Paisley wipes a tear of joy from his wrinkled face. 'I love happy continuances.'

We ponder the fairytales. 'Both stories are about being cold and not having a family, a home.'

'And what do ye think the metaphor might be?' asks Paisley.

'Life is a Cold Winter?' we ask.

Paisley nods. 'That's a good answer, but in Helen's case the metaphor needs to be spelled out even more. Maybe, *Life is a Cold and Desolate Winter's Day Where We're All Alone, Unsheltered, and Unloved – but Hopeful that in the End, a Family Will Take Us in.*'

'Oh, yes, we see. In both stories, a family took the person – or duck – in.'

Plaid explains. 'Yes, and hope is an important aspect of the metaphor. It's what kept Helen tied into the metaphor. By placing yer hope in the future or in the past, ye are no longer living in the present, which robs ye of the Divine energy to exist in the moment. It put Helen's energy on someone or something else to change things for her, so she had less energy to change it herself.'

'Aye,' adds Paisley. 'Yer society, church, and schools often dangle that hope in front of humans like a carrot, and reaching for it is what keeps them ever striving – and into that metaphor.' He points to our tablet. 'Now it's time for ye to write.'

*With your **Wand** write your answers to this question: 'Which stories, songs, fairytales, or movies did you resonate with as a young person?' Remember especially those you loved or that touched you in a deep way. Free write for 10 minutes or longer, taking as much time as you need.*

'There's one more question,' says Plaid when we finish writing. 'It's similar to the last one. What books, stories, songs, or movies have touched ye as an adult?'

Some thoughts come immediately to mind, and we begin to write.

What books, stories, songs, or movies have touched you as an adult? Write.
Take as much time as you need.

When we finish, Plaid is waiting to show us another photograph. 'This is Celine, a beautiful lady. Lovely silvery hair.' He touches her hair in the photo with a knobby finger. 'Celine was an executive in a big corporation, had lots of responsibility, and was very effective in her job.'

'But something was amiss, shall we say?' Paisley gnome tilts his head to look us directly in the eye. 'Like most humans, her bad days were sometimes very bad. When we asked her about songs and movies, she gave us an earful!'

Flowered cups his pointy ears with his curved hands, and they all laugh.

'Ye see, when things were difficult for Celine, she would watch Rambo movies on her video player,' Paisley continues. 'We asked her why she did that. She said that Rambo would get backed into a corner and come out fighting.'

'So we asked her,' says Plaid gnome, 'if it made her feel good to see someone else come out fighting when she felt like the underdog herself. And she said yes.'

'And what was the metaphor?' we ask.

'Quite simple,' says Plaid. *Life is a Rambo Movie.* It was the image that defined her life when things were most difficult. Her tough life situation, a male-dominant environment, would force Celine into a place of fear. She operated on the basis of fight or flight, rather than love and compassion, which is where things can change. She felt that the only way she could cope with things was to operate like Rambo. And she was very surprised it was her life metaphor!'

'I can imagine!' We ponder whether there are any particular movies or stories that make us feel better on a bad day.

'Many people try to solve their problems from a place of fear,' adds Paisley, 'which only postpones the problem. Whereas if they operated from love, they wouldn't find themselves forced into a corner.'

'More tea?' Flowered gnome has brought a fresh pot and begun to refill the cups.

Plaid continues. 'So look at yer list of movies and songs and fairytales. Does anything have a charge to it, a sort of glow? Ye know, the one that sticks out more than the others?'

Look at your list and see which of the titles jumps out at you. Mark these.

'Let's take a gander at yer lists,' says Paisley.

We turn the tablet so they can see the ones we have marked. On the bad-day list are *Life is One Job after Another* and *Life is Having to Constantly Stay after School.* On the stories and fairytale list is the Greek myth of Sisyphus, who was destined to eternally push a boulder uphill, with the constant threat of it rolling back and crushing him.

'Ah, ye see how these fit together?' says Plaid gnome. 'No end to responsibilities or punishment. I suggest *Life is a Sisyphus Myth* as yer old metaphor, the one that operates when ye are having a bad day. Ye find yerself continually rolling that boulder uphill, and never getting out from under it.'

The weight of it resonates inside. 'That's a crummy metaphor,' we say, 'but it sure does feel true.'

Dear reader, take plenty of time with this step. Look at your list of bad-day metaphors and your lists of stories, fairytales, movies, songs. Do you see a pattern? Look for an image that resonates inside you – how it feels when things are not going well, or when you're having a bad day. Choose one.

If you need additional assistance with this step, reread what is written in The Book of Life, noting the examples given there. Perhaps one of those metaphors rings true for you.

When you have found one, write it down on a separate sheet of paper and take it out of your writing tablet. It should follow the format 'Life is a _____.'

'And how has that metaphor affected yer life?' asks Plaid. The other gnomes pull up their stools, so that they are sitting quite close. Their breath is in our face, sweet and warm. 'Yes, yes,' says Paisley.

'We wish to know,' says Flowered.

'The Sisyphus myth? Well, we seem to take a lot of responsibility for other people, especially our family. We've tried very hard to help them have better lives, and we've worried about them a lot. We don't want it to feel like a burden, but it often does. And we imagine they can feel the heaviness in us.'

'Aye, yes, they can,' nods Paisley. 'They wish ye wouldn't worry about them so.'

'Sometimes, no matter what we do or how hard we try, things pile up on us, and we can never get out from under the tasks and duties of our life. It used to be that way all the time, but now it only happens when things are especially difficult.'

'Ah! The metaphor takes over,' says Plaid.

'And ye lose that sense of joy and peace,' says Flowered.

How has the old metaphor affected your life? In your writing tablet, make a list of these categories, leaving three or four lines between the categories so that you have room to make notes: Divine Purpose, Relationships, Creativity, Health, Career, Spiritual Focus, Outlook, Prosperity.

Beside each category, write the effects of your old metaphor on each of these areas of your life. Allow yourself at least 15 minutes to do this task.

Paisley is ready with a question. 'And we suppose ye don't wish to keep that crummy and unworthy metaphor? Otherwise ye wouldn't be here?'

'Absolutely.' We nod. 'We can't wait to pick a new one. But we wish to ask something first: If we get a new metaphor, what happens to our karma – you know, our past wrongdoings, or even those good things we've done for people?'

The Karma in Your Garage

'Ah, karma!' says Plaid. He winks at Paisley and Flowered.

'A fine question,' says Paisley. He tilts his head back, savoring the last drops in his cup, where honey oozes at the bottom.

'Karma,' says Plaid, 'is one of those belief systems that can get ye tangled in the briar. It has roots in ancient Hinduism and other old-world religions, from a time when people saw life and death as a continuing cycle, with little chance of escape. The modern version of this belief – subscribed to by what ye call New Agers – says that Earth is a cosmic school. Ye are here to learn yer lessons and work off yer bad deeds. In some future lifetime ye might work it all off. And when ye do something good, the angels record it on the great balance sheet in the sky.'

We hold out our cup for Flowered to pour us more tea. 'Our friends say we are always paying for our past deeds, and that we should behave well toward others in order to create good karma for ourselves.'

'Otherwise ye come back as a gnome,' laughs Paisley.

'Or an ant or a bug!' says Flowered, leaning close to our ear. 'Although, I don't think that would be so bad.'

'Oh, we don't, either.' We smile into Flowered's cheery face. 'Not since being in the Ever-Present.'

'Behaving kindly toward others is a good thing,' says Plaid emphatically.

Flowered and Paisley nod in agreement.

'But if we've done terrible things in a past life, are we relegated to lifetimes of misery?' Even one lifetime of misery seems like a very long time.

When ye live in Is, the past loses its hold on ye.

'When ye live in Is, the past loses its hold on ye. Yer life is full of treasures,' says Flowered, spreading his arms wide to include everything in the cave – the quilt-covered beds, pictures of the Divine Mothers, the odd set of flowerpots, and the red velvet caps. He blows a kiss to the picture of the Divine Mother in the flowered dress.

'Here on the island ye are letting things go,' says Paisley. 'If ye subscribe to the beliefs about karma, it will indeed affect ye. But if ye should wish to work off the karma and move beyond that belief system, forgiveness and especially forgiving yerself is a good place to start. Realizing that there is only one Divine Self allows ye to understand the Golden Rule and the Law of Karma. If ye are hurting anyone, ye are really hurting yerself.

'It requires being truthful with yerself,' he continues, 'being willing to look at yer past deeds. This brings ye into a place of integrity, where ye can forgive yerself by letting go of yer grief and thoughts of misdoings – offering them to the Divine. Being here on the island is evidence that ye are ready to leave behind that belief system and live from a place of Divinity.'

'When ye have seen yerself as Divinity, ye move beyond the effects of beliefs,' adds Flowered, his eyes beaming love at us. 'Ye step beyond karma. There are no more karma collisions!'

'This is where yer new metaphor comes in,' says Plaid. 'The old metaphor latches onto ye, to prevent ye from enjoying peace and joy and understanding. It creates a field of energy about ye, like a hologram, that becomes very limiting. Ye have to let go of a lot of past – and past karma – in order to live on the Isle of Is. Living in Is is about being in the present, not being eternally attached to some ancient wrongdoing.'

'As permanent residents of Is, we have no karma in our garage.' Paisley beams, nodding toward the quaint flowerpots.

'Nor in our cave, either!' says Flowered.

'But you have flowers growing in your cave, and there's hardly enough light!' we exclaim.

Plaid touches our shoulder. 'Life happens, dear traveler, when ye let go of the past and future. Everything flourishes.'

The Vein of God

'Oh, it's time to visit the Vein of God!' says Flowered, jumping up from the table and dancing a bit of a jig.

'Don't you mean the Vein of Gold?' we ask.

'Oh, no! It's even more valuable than gold.' Plaid dons his red hat.

'We'll need a torch to get to the Vein. Mind if I have that?' Paisley takes the paper with our old metaphor on it, wraps it tightly into a cone, and sets the end on fire. 'Ye won't be needing this any more.' He uses the old metaphor to light a tightly wound bundle of twigs, then tosses the burning slip of paper into the pot-bellied stove, where it flares up with a brilliant flash of light.

Plaid pauses to appreciate the sight. 'The old metaphors are happy to exhaust themselves in the flame. They enjoy the freedom, too.'

The old metaphors enjoy the freedom, too.

As we turn to leave, we spot a piece of parchment tacked on the wall near the stove. It's a To-Do list, but the word 'Do' has been scratched out and replaced by 'Be.'

TO-BE LIST

1. Forget yer troubles.

2. Come on.

3. Be happy.

'Everybody ready?' Paisley pushes open a stone door at the back of the cavern.

Plaid takes the lead, followed by Flowered and Paisley. The torch creates a bright halo around Plaid's red hat. We feel as though we are following a procession of angels.

As we walk, we notice little sparkles on the ground, rose-colored and lime and aqua. 'Are we walking on the Vein of God?' we ask.

Paisley shakes his head. 'This is just part of the beauty that gets us there.'

The deeper into the cave we go, the more vibrant the sparkles become. They run up onto the walls, creating ever-widening trails of colored gems – citrine, peridot, opal, aquamarine, rose quartz. It is as though the walls are lit from within. We pause to touch a ribbon of rose quartz. 'It's so beautiful!'

'Aye,' says Paisley, his head bobbing.

But the gnomes are moving on ahead, and we run to catch up. Soon, the passage opens into a circular space with gems in the walls and a pool in the center, which contains fist-sized nuggets of the colored stones. A myriad of gems spills from the walls like diamonds. An opening in the ceiling of the cave channels sunlight directly into the pool. We gasp at the beauty of the light cascading onto the colored gems.

'This is the Vein of God?' We gesture at the pool and the walls.

'It is, it is,' says Flowered. 'Very few humans make it this far.' He takes our hand in his, which is crinkly and small, both wizened and childlike at the same time. He leads us around the circle, showing us the gems embedded in the walls. Some of the stones are lit up in tiny niches.

Flowered stops beside the pool, which is actually a font with water bubbling up from underneath. It is a font of energy, with light molecules floating around.

Paisley leans close to our ear. 'Divinity has carved the stones ye see here – each gem is carved into its own individuality. One of them is just right for ye.'

'Ye see the shelves we made for some of the gems?' Plaid points to the niches. 'Other travelers chose these gems from the font of the Vein of God.'

'Look,' says Paisley, reaching into a nearby niche. 'This peridot was Sylvia's. Can ye feel this vibration?' He places it in our hands. 'Hers was the metaphor, *Life is a Heavenly Garden.*'

As we hold the pale green stone, a feeling of deep peace comes over us, and the sensation of standing in a lush glen. 'Oh, yes! We feel it!'

Paisley takes the peridot from us, placing a pale pink crystal in our hands. 'Now feel this one. At first, David's metaphor was *Life is Holding the Hand of God,* but we helped him see that it was his own hand he was holding.'

This stone immediately opens our heart. 'Oh my!' we say, handing the rose quartz back to Paisley. 'It's so powerful. Just from getting a new metaphor?'

'Yes, dear one,' says Flowered. 'The metaphor carries its own vibration. Think of ye old metaphor, based on the Sisyphus myth. What kind of vibration did that one carry?'

Yes, dear one, the metaphor carries its own vibration.

'Very heavy! Hard work and plodding effort, that's what that metaphor was.'

'Tis true. And a vibration that weighed ye down,' says Flowered.

Paisley eases a large clear crystal into our hands. 'What do ye feel now?'

We hold it in our palm, closing our eyes. This one vibrates with the sensation of light, as though it would lift us to the skies to be among the clouds. At the same time, we feel very connected to the Earth beneath our feet. We try to put it into words. 'It seems to be heavenly, yet connected to this place, too. It's as though the waves of energy are flowing through us in both directions.'

'Tis an apt description,' says Flowered gnome, nodding to the others. 'Michael chose the metaphor *Life is a Paradise Island,* inspired, ye think, by the Isle of Is?' All three chuckle and beam at us. 'On *this* paradise island, ye experience the air, the water, the trees, the earth – everything – as Divine.'

'Each person was able to put their metaphor into words that resonate with them personally,' says Plaid gnome. 'And that is exactly yer task.'

'After ye choose a gem, of course,' says Paisley, pointing to the font. 'Here, sit on the edge of the pool. Let yer feet dangle in the water.'

We take off our shoes and sit down on the damp cave floor, easing our feet into the most alive water we have ever experienced. It seems to send gentle currents of energy up our legs and into our body. Wishing to savor the experience, we take a few moments to breathe, relax, and feel what is happening.

'Here's yer quiver,' says Plaid, handing it to us. 'Ye'll need yer tongs and dipper – they will assist ye in picking just the right stone.'

As we open the quiver, the dipper and tongs jump out and land on the rock beside us.

'They are eager to help ye, we see,' says Flowered, a twinkle in his eye.

We take the tongs and dipper into our lap, then close our eyes and invite them to assist us in choosing the best metaphor for us, one that will allow us to acknowledge ourselves as Divine.

As you prepare to choose a new metaphor, find an illuminated place. Perhaps a cozy spot inside your house where the sunlight or a favorite lamp spills its rays onto your lap. Or perhaps in Nature by a favorite tree or on a favorite bench. Choose a place that puts you most in touch with Beauty, God, Spirit.

*Bring your **Wand** and writing tablet into this space. Also bring an implement that will serve as a dipper – something to scoop up the Divine Presence all around you. This might be a bowl or a cup.*

How would you most like to see your life?

*Once in this place, enter the **Well**. Close your eyes and take a few relaxed breaths. Breathe, relax, and feel. How would you most like to see your life? A life in which you experience yourself as most creative, most beautiful, most Divine. Allow yourself to touch in to what resonates with you. Allow the Most High to show up.*

Hold your dipper in your hands. Invite your new life metaphor to present itself to you. Visualize this metaphor choosing you and filling your dipper.

When an inspiration comes to you, write it down. Sit quietly and invite any others that might resonate with you to present themselves as well. Do not engage the mind in searching. Simply allow a metaphor or metaphors to show up. It may be a metaphor you have read about in this chapter.

If more than one have appeared, choose one.

When we open our eyes, one particular gem is winking at us – an aquamarine, palest blue, the color of water and sky. It feels perfect to us. Leaning forward, we use the tongs to extract it from the font. Then we place it in the dipper, which we hold before us to show the gnomes.

'Ah, perfection!' 'Such beauty!' 'It suits ye to a tee,' say the gnomes.

We take the stone into our hands.

'Sit with yer stone for a while,' says Paisley. 'Don't ye mind us one teeny bit.' The gnomes begin sweeping the circular space with straw brooms, and as they do, the sparkles dance off the floor.

We close our eyes and again breathe, relax, feel. The gem pulses in our hands like a baby's heart.

After a few minutes, Flowered whispers in our ear. 'Allow the perfect metaphor to come to ye. Then write it down with yer Wand.'

An inspiration comes right away, and we write it down: *Life is an Ocean of Being.*

'Tell us, tell us,' say the gnomes, gathering around.

We read the metaphor to them. 'It was the blue that inspired it, and the heavenly experience of sky and water when we lay on the rock in the Ocean of Being. We wish to have this in our life always.'

'Tis lovely beyond description,' agrees Flowered. 'I love the Ocean of Being.'

The other gnomes put a hand on each of Flowered's shoulders. 'Tis lovely, indeed,' says Paisley. 'But tell us more. What will yer life be like with this new metaphor?'

What will your life be like in the new metaphor?

We consider the question. 'Peaceful. We can always return to the depths of the ocean, and the light, happy movement of ocean breezes. Whatever is happening in our life, we can lie back and feel ourselves supported by the rock, by Earth. We can communicate with the beings of Nature, like the white fish, to remind us of our Divinity.'

'Excellent,' says Paisley, and the others nod in agreement. 'We think ye have a new metaphor.'

*Take a few moments to consider your new metaphor. Does it allow you to acknowledge and experience your own Divinity? Does it allow you to experience life as Divine? If so, then proceed to the directions below. If not, return to the **Well** and ask that an even more uplifting and grace-filled metaphor come to you.*

Now write down what the new metaphor means to you – your thoughts and feelings about life in the new metaphor. What does the new metaphor allow your life to be like? These particulars will assist you in entering the reality of the metaphor in your daily life. Use the same categories of your life that you considered in the last writing exercise: Divine Purpose, Relationships, Creativity, Health, Career, Spiritual Focus, Outlook, Prosperity. How will the new metaphor affect these areas of your life?

The next task will take some preparation. You will create a collage that represents the new metaphor. You will need a sheet of poster board, and also images in magazines that resonate with the new metaphor and the beauty you feel. If you do not have access to magazines with uplifting images, ask friends, a doctor's office, or a local library – often they have some they are ready to discard – or purchase one or two that will contain images for your metaphor.

Make the time to do this process, for the rewards will be great. By creating a new image that you will see every day, you will begin to take the new metaphor into your Self and into your life.

Do not think too much as you make your selection of images for the collage. Keep the mind relaxed and at peace. Simply choose images that you like. If you find yourself selecting images that you 'think' do not fit the metaphor, do not worry. Allow whatever images that show up to show up. You may find that the images will direct you to refine or redefine your new metaphor.

Once you have selected the images and cut them out, affix them to the poster board with glue or tape. You may also choose to add a few words to the collage; however, it is important to rely largely on images to exemplify the new metaphor rather than words.

When you have created your collage of the new metaphor, find someone to share it with. Post it where you will see it every day.

'We are pleased with yer metaphor and with yer Self,' says Plaid gnome. 'Are ye pleased, too?'

'Oh, yes!'

'We will hold yer gemstone here in the Vein of God to inspire others who come this way,' Plaid continues, taking it from us gently. 'It shall remain here, vibrating, acknowledging yer Divinity throughout the created and uncreated Universes.'

Keep the words and images of the new metaphor in your heart.

'Keep the words and images of the new metaphor in yer heart,' adds

Flowered. 'And when ye get home, post images of the new metaphor everywhere. Will ye do that?'

'Yes, we will!'

'Good. Now, it is our task to point ye toward the Cascades of Compassion.' Plaid heads down a passage that we have not noticed till now, which veers off in a direction opposite to that of the gnomes' cavern.

At the end of the passage, he opens a rock door onto a gentle slope that is near the bottom of Mount Metaphor. 'Use yer keys,' says Paisley.

'And remember us here.' Flowered puts his hand on our heart.

'Oh, we will, we will. Bye now!' We wave to them with adoration. Heading off down the slope, we hear tiny voices in the forest and feel a connection to everything.

10 | *Cascades of Compassion & Drops of Devotion*

The hurt ye embrace becomes joy.
Call it to your arms where it can change.

J. Rumi

The view from the trail opens wide to the end of the slope. Beside the trail are morning glory, yellow and red hibiscus, and frangipani trees, whose white clusters fill the air with a heavenly fragrance. We suspect that the gnomes have done some gardening. About halfway down, we see a small sign that says, **Magic Is Afoot**. Tucked into a nearby branch is a worn boot, in a size perfect for a gnome. Inside is the nest of a swiftlet, who darts in and out to feed four small mouths. She sweetly chirps in recognition of our presence.

It is an easy hike, and we are filled with joy. At the bottom of the slope is a clump of spreading mango trees; built around one is a bench made of branches. The fruit is ready to be picked, and we partake of luscious mangoes as we seat ourselves to enjoy the shade. We take out our map and keys. Three keys are left: one shows a winding stream; another, a sand castle; and a third, a waterfall. In our hands, the key with the image of a waterfall begins to pulse. We hold up the map. A trail is being etched down Mount Metaphor and into a pine forest, where the path winds to a rock ledge and falling water.

It looks to be some distance away, so we lean against the tree for a short rest. No sooner have we closed our eyes than we hear Plaid's voice: 'Take yer new metaphor into meditation,' he says. 'It will redefine the electrons and photons and create the metaphor in yer life.'

'Show us how,' we say silently.

Plaid continues to talk, his voice floating on the wind.

*Go to the **Well**. As you breathe and relax and feel, ask to be taken to the deep peace inside you. If this does not come easily, set down the past and future, step into a meadow, and into the light. Be in the light, without calling forth the personalities.*

When you can feel the peace that resides within you, call up an image of your new metaphor. Say the metaphor silently to yourself. Then call forth images that you associate with the new metaphor – images of the ocean, a garden, a park, a rainforest, whatever suits the metaphor. Allow all your senses to be awakened – sight, sound, smell, taste, touch. Look deeply at what you might see in the new metaphor, perhaps birds, flowers, children, or colors. Notice the smallest details. Listen carefully for what you might hear. Smell the aromas of the surroundings of your metaphor. Touch those things that would be present in the metaphor, feeling their textures.

Remain in the Well with your dreamscape of the new metaphor for 15 minutes or longer.

We open our eyes, invigorated by the images we have called forth. We have the feeling that we were indeed in that place. All of our senses verified the experience of being in the new metaphor.

'Ye have just entered the field where dreams become reality,' says Plaid. 'Within this force field, yer emotions and thoughts create what it is ye wish to manifest. They have an impact on even the most distant stars. In the Well we get in touch with the power that's in the Universe. The closer ye are to that source, the more powerful the manifestation becomes.'

Ye have entered the field where dreams become reality.

'And this source would be the Ocean of Being?'

'Indeed,' says Plaid. 'In meditation ye take yer new metaphor into Being. At the Vein of God, the metaphor was also set in gemstone. Now it's yer joy to establish the metaphor in yer everyday life.'

The images in the meditation were vivid, and we have the sense that we have indeed rearranged the electrons and photons. We feel exhilarated by our visit to the Well and are ready to head down the trail.

Quoth the Raven Evermore

It is a pleasant hike through tall fir trees, whose regal bearing reminds us of kings and queens. The sun beams down, and brightly colored lorikeets twitter as they dip gaily around us. The scent of pine reminds us to breathe deeply as we go.

We notice that we are having thoughts of Mother, Jane, and home, though not as many as before. We are not so bombarded by thoughts and feelings. The new metaphor has brought more spaciousness, and we are able to touch in and identify with Divinity. Yet the spaciousness makes it easier to see that some debris still exists. Old feelings arise – feelings we've carried around for a long time and don't need any more – useless karmic debris. As we walk, feelings of helplessness about the lives of those we love come to the surface. But we are able to breathe and feel them without getting too caught up in worry and doubt.

After some time, we stop beside the trail to rest. The gnomes gave us seeds, nuts, and dried fruit for our hike, and sitting in the sunshine we savor each bite. We marvel that anything could taste so good.

Feeling replenished, we pack the remaining food back into the quiver. When we look up, a satiny black bird – a raven – is perched on a rock watching us, her dark brown eyes luminous. The sun falls on her feathers, creating a purplish metallic sheen. We nod to the bird and toss her a handful of seeds. She hops onto the trail to nibble the seeds with her curved stout bill, then returns to her perch, where she continues to observe our movements.

Unrolling the map, we see that the waterfall is just a short walk away. It has been a splendid day thus far, and we feel intensely present. We are excited about the changes we feel in our awareness and our sense of connection to all of Nature.

Waving goodbye to the raven, we begin hiking again. But as we walk, the raven lifts into the air and flies in circles around us, swooping and calling. We watch her as closely as she watched us, noting her beautiful wedged tail, the ruff of feathers at her neck, and her many dives and tumbles.

After a short while, she lands on the trail behind us. 'Prruk-prruk, kra-kra.'

The new metaphor has brought more spaciousness.

The sounds come from deep in her throat. We turn to see her hopping down the trail as though hiking toward the waterfall with us. Delighted, we laugh! After a few minutes, the raven takes to the air again, circling high above. Then she lands on the trail behind us once more, her nubby black feet splaying the dust as she walks. We are touched by her antics and by her friendship. The raven has reaffirmed the pervasiveness of the Ever-Present, and we take the occasion to acknowledge the movement of Spirit in all things.

In the distance we hear the rumble of water on rocks. As we near the falls, the rumble becomes a gentle gushing. Then we see it: Water cascades over one rock ledge and onto another, forming a waterfall. The spray created by the falls dissipates into the air, creating a myriad of prisms. On the ledge behind the waterfall is a space where one could sit or stand.

Interested in exploring the ledge, we lean our quiver against a tree and carefully pick our way over stones that are slippery with foam and moss. We step through the cascade and onto the rock ledge. Here behind the waterfall it is cool and moist. To one side is a small clear pool formed by water dripping from above. Each drop releases itself into the pool with complete abandon, joyously uniting with the water below.

We sit down behind the falls and close our eyes, feeling the vibration of the surging water and the spray on our skin. We slip easily into meditation, setting aside past and future, and entering the light, knowing this will bring even greater clarity. Images and thoughts of the past enter our awareness. Most of these come and go, until we become aware of blobs of darkness floating in our mind's eye.

Uncomfortable with this image, we open our eyes. We have not seen this before. We close our eyes again; the amorphous shapes continue to float inside our awareness, as though drifting up from a swamp at the bottom of our mental screen. Then we notice that they have wiggly legs – and faces. The word that comes to mind is *ghoulies*. Small wriggling ghoulies inside us! How can this be?

Troubled, we stand up behind the cascading water and look around. The pool has grown murky, the bottom no longer visible. This sends a shiver up our spine. Discomfited, we step outside the waterfall and find a rock some distance away, where we can sit beside a pine tree and gaze up at the falls and the coursing water. What was this experience about, and where did the ghoulies come from? The ghoulies repulse us, and we are unsure if we wish to enter the Well again.

A shuffling in the fir tree causes us to look up. Our companion the raven gazes down at us.

We wonder if the raven can speak to us, and if she can help. Surely she, too, is a member of the Ever-Present.

'Quork,' says the raven, flying to a lower branch. 'Yes, I do talk, and I can help. Is-is is my name.'

'Is-is? Like the Egyptian goddess Isis?'

'Yes, but the correct pronunciation of *Is-is* has been lost over time.' The raven swoops even closer. 'Also lost is the knowledge that Is-is is the Divine one, the only one, the greatest of gods and goddesses, maker of the sunrise, light-giver of Heaven, God-mother, the most mighty one, giver of life. I am that – in the form of a humble bird. This Divinity is not about ego. It simply is-is.'

Divinity is not about ego. It simply is-is.

We shake our head in amazement. 'We did not know that the goddess was all that. It seems that history has not been so kind to Isis. And are you she?'

'I am.' Is-is lifts her head as though to revel in her own beauty. 'I am the Divine one, lady of Heaven, queen of the earth. And so are you.'

We laugh. 'Perhaps – just perhaps – we are Divine. But we are not all that.'

'You are a great power. Not the ego part of you, not the part that wants and needs and acquires and loses. The Divine You is great love and great presence.'

'Then why do we continue to identify with our ego, our worries and feelings? And what happened just now during meditation? That was scary.'

'Here on the Island of Is-is, you have received wonderful tools for living as a human in the physical world. Even though you have these tools, the past may bubble up from time to time. Persevere, beloved one. Continue to use the tools. It is residual debris that has surfaced, not Divinity. The pool is murky, but it can easily be made clear again.'

'But why would this come up during meditation? We thought meditation was the way to experience the Ever-Present, not the past.'

'Meditation is a process of continual clearing. It allows what is inside you, unfinished, unresolved, to surface so that it might be released.' Is-is, the lady of life, flaps her wings in a motion of liberation.

We smile at her, entertaining the idea that the goddess Isis has indeed shown up to instruct us.

'Be present with whatever arises,' she continues, her brown eyes focused intensely on us. 'When uncomfortable feelings or images come in meditation, this is where people may leave the tools they have, the knowing they have. They may stop meditating completely, due to this discomfort. This is when the old metaphor fights to hang on for its egoic life, wishing to delude you.'

'What do you mean exactly, to be present with it?'

'We mean to bring your loving awareness to whatever is there. Breathe into it. Feel it. Observe it. Send loving thoughts and feelings to it. Often, humans try to deny their feelings or turn away from them. However, feelings can only be released if they are experienced.'

Bring your loving awareness to whatever is there.

We think of the metaphor of Sisyphus, and the constant work of pushing a boulder uphill. Living in the old metaphor did feel like being in a swamp – a swamp filled with ghoulies – stuck in a pattern and unable to get out. Feeling murky and beset by dark spirits fits the pattern rather well. 'We've discovered ghoulies inside us,' we confess.

'This is very good,' says Is-is. 'They have been there all along, taking up residence within a part of your Presence, using up your electricity, drinking your water. But now you know they are there and can release them. Being consciously present with them is what will let them go. The ghoulies cannot exist in your Presence, just as the past cannot exist in the Now, just as 3:30 cannot exist at 4 o'clock.'

She pauses before speaking again. 'Embrace the ghoulies, dear one. Call them to your arms where they can change.'

A Ghoulie Is Only a Ghoulie

'Will you show us how?'

She nods. 'It is a technique that the Buddha talked about, to call up anything and everything that's uncomfortable in order to clean out your inner closet. You have experienced this process while on the island: breathe, relax, feel. Now we will help you understand how to use the process when images or feelings appear in meditation.' Is-is covers her eyes with one shiny black wing, showing us that we are to close our eyes.

Presence Practice. *Eyes closed, allow yourself to go to the* **Well**. *Bring your awareness to your breath.*

1. Breathe.

2. Relax.

3. Feel.

Take a few moments with each aspect of the process, then return to the beginning and repeat the steps several times.

Now call up an uncomfortable thought or feeling – perhaps one that has arisen in meditation, or one that you have experienced in the past few days. Allow yourself to experience that thought or feeling in your body.

Add two steps to the process:

4. Observe the sensations. Allow your mind to notice and observe the thought or feeling. What are the sensations that accompany it? Where are the sensations located in your body? How big is the area? Does it have a color, a shape? Do not engage in judgment about the sensations by telling yourself they are too painful, that they have been there forever (a thought associated with the past), or that it will never go away (a thought associated with the future). Simply be in the present moment with the sensation. Breathing, relaxing, feeling, and observing.

5. Finally, bring increased Divine Presence to the sensations by embracing them with love. Think love, feel love. With your loving awareness, embrace the area of your body where the sensations are located, as though this were your child.

Repeat these steps for a total of 15 minutes or longer. When you have finished, take up your **Wand** *and write.*

'What happened to the ghoulies?' asks Is-is when we look up from our writing.

We laugh, amazed by the experience. 'They continued to float up, two or three at a time, and as we observed them and sent them love, they dissolved. They became one with the light and drifted away.'

'Are there any ghoulies left?' asks the raven.

'Yes, a few, we think. Will they go away if we continue to do Presence Practice?'

'They will. You can also talk to them. Ask them what they are and if there is anything they need from you besides your awareness and your love. The more you go to the Well, and the more aware you are of your Divinity, the more the ghoulies and other discomforts subside. The ghoulies have come in the process of casting off the old metaphor. They want to drag you back to your old life metaphor.'

'Some people say that one should accept what is. Is this the same thing as Presence Practice?'

Raven shakes her head, ruffling her feathers. 'No, it is not. You are bringing Presence, or Divinity, into what is – it's not an acceptance of what is. That is a mistaken idea. Acceptance suggests gritting your teeth and bearing it. Rather, this is an active process – a process of recognizing Being and Presence that are there all the time. Through Presence Practice, you open yourself to the flow of love and, therefore, flow compassion toward yourself. Allow your consciousness to be aware of that underlying Presence. It is always there.'

Is-is gestures toward the waterfall with her beak. 'These are the Cascades of Compassion. See the rainbows all about?'

We look up, astonished at the bright arcs of color that now imbue this place – a transformation from prisms to rainbows. 'Look at the double rainbows!' we exclaim.

'When you recognize the truth of what is that underlies everything, that is Divinity recognizing Divinity. Bringing Presence into what is, awakens the Divine that underlies Presence. It has a multiplier effect, like a double rainbow. That's why we call it *is-is.*'

Bringing Presence into what is, awakens the Divine.

'It's so beautiful!'

'And it is constantly flowing. It is a metaphor for compassion in your own life. Flow love and compassion toward yourself with the fullness and the power of the cascades.' The raven gestures again. 'Go. Visit the waterfall once more.'

The Quantum Pool

We make our way across the stones to the rock ledge, then step under the falls as though behind a curtain. The water tumbles all around us. The rainbows are even more brilliantly colored when we look from inside, and the once-murky pool is again pristine. Water continues to drip slowly into the pool.

Approaching the pool, we are fascinated by the action of the drops on the surface. Each drop reflects the essence of infinity. We become aware that drops are like waves in the ocean – they are merely aspects of the totality of Being.

As we peer into the water, the pool transforms into the font in the cavern with its many-colored gems. The hues of the gems vibrate inside the pool.

Curious to know if they are real, we reach into the water to touch the aquamarine. To our amazement, it comes out easily in our hand. We turn the stone over to examine its facets. On one facet is an image of the Vein of God, where the gnomes, brooms in hand, are grinning and waving. We smile at their cheery faces and wave back. Another facet is a window to the Ocean of Being, where night stars are reflected on its surface. The white fish, brighter than the other sparks of light, flicks its tail in acknowledgment and dives into the deep. Yet another facet is a portal to the Pool of (Ac)Knowledge, where the ferryman's face has come into view. All the pools have become one.

'Oh!' A gasp of delight escapes our mouth.

The ferryman grins. 'All these manifestations of the Divine have come in different forms only to make your trip more educational, more enjoyable. And the Divine enjoys the play. Shakespeare got it partially right, but ye are not merely a player. Ye are the orchestra. Ye are the conductor, the choreographer, and the costume designer. Ye are the play. And everyone in the audience is Divinely *ye*. There is truly no separation.'

'And we are the ferryman, too, carrying us back and forth to the stage?'

This brings a big laugh. 'Do ye know where ye are?' he asks.

'At the Cascades of Compassion,' we say.

'Aye, and the Drops of Devotion. Cascades and drops – both contain the essence of all things.'

'Is-is told us that we are to flow compassion toward ourselves,' we say.

'Indeed, ye are. And devotion as well. '

'We don't understand. Isn't compassion something we feel and do to help other people? And isn't devotion being dedicated to God?'

'Compassion as feeling what someone else feels and helping them out, and devotion to God – these are wonderful, but this is more than that. Think ye, what does God need with devotion? Compassion and devotion are Divine qualities, and they are essentially the same. Both involve flowing love to yourself, and in this way, ye increase the flow of Spirit into your personality, and from there, out into the world.'

'And how do we do that – flow love toward our self?'

'By loving yourself in all your thoughts and actions. By visiting the Well, and acknowledging and reconnecting with the Divine being that ye are.'

Love yourself in all your thoughts and actions.

The idea that loving our self is the same thing as compassion and devotion stuns us for a moment. 'But focusing our love on our self – isn't this selfish, and self-centered?'

The ferryman shakes his head. 'When ye are filled with Spirit, it bubbles to ye and through ye and into the world. Ye flow the excess. There's more than enough to go around for everyone. It's limitless. Ye *become* compassion and devotion. This is a sight better, don't ye think, than approaching everything in life from a place of inadequacy or lack?

'The extent to which ye can be devoted to the self and compassionate toward the self,' he continues, 'is in direct proportion to the amount of Divinity ye allow yourself to experience. There is *doing* compassion, when ye flow love toward others, but this is not that. This is not *doing* compassion or *doing* devotion. Rather, by loving yourself, ye increase the flow and vibration of compassion and devotion. Compassion is a by-product of being in a state of Being. It is an energy stream of Divinity that flows through ye.'

'And we might practice this when ghoulies show up?'

'Aye, and when ye wake up, when ye sit down to eat, when ye go to bed at night . . .'

'In other words, all the time.' We laugh.

Add **Presence Practice** *to your daily life, flowing love to yourself by doing the five-step process:*

1. *Breathe.*
2. *Relax.*
3. *Feel.*
4. *Observe the sensations in your body.*
5. *Embrace the sensations, your body, and yourself with love.*

Do this anytime . . .

. . . you have a bad feeling about yourself.

. . . you make a judgment about yourself.

CD Track 5:

Presence Practice

. . . you have an uncomfortable feeling about anything.

You may wish to use the first three steps — breathe, relax, feel — to bring yourself into the present moment in an ongoing way. Use it while waiting in traffic, waiting in line, trying to fall asleep at night — indeed, any time you are caught up in your thoughts or emotions — and throughout your day. Do it from a place of non-judgment and unconditional love.

We have more questions about compassion. 'Ferryman, what can we do when a person or animal we love is hurting — when we wish to help others in need?'

'If a beloved animal were dying,' says the ferryman, as an image of an animal we have known appears in his arms, 'flow love to it, allowing it to be at ease as its spirit prepares to pass on. This is much more powerful and helpful than allowing yourself to be sunk in grief or fear. Your bad feelings draw energy from the dying animal because they are of a low vibration, whereas your love infuses the animal with love. If bad feelings arise, simply shift your focus to the feeling of love. Love will prevail — even as ye feel fear or grief — because love is a higher vibration. Being in a state of love — this is true compassion.'

Being in a state of love — this is true compassion.

We think of Auntie May's surgery and Mother's fear of being burgled. 'And this works with people, too?'

'Indeed, it does. Claude, one of our travelers, expressed grief about being estranged from his mother. We invited him to sit in silence and flow love and Divine Presence to her. At first he had difficulty with this concept and doubts of its effectiveness. Yet he was open to putting it into practice, as all else had failed. When he returned to his house after visiting the island, a package containing a gift and a personal note was waiting from his mother. It was his mother's first communication in more than five years.'

'That's a wonderful story,' we say. 'And a miracle. We think it might be difficult to do, especially if you feel resentment or anger toward someone.'

'In fact, it is easy to do,' the ferryman says gently, 'once you get your mind out of the way. And it does work miracles. Many indigenous people know the truth of this. Among Australian Aborigines, for example, when someone awakes from a dream where another person is angry with them, the spiritual leader of the clan gathers the dreamer, the one dreamed of, and the entire community to open a discussion to resolve the situation. The Aborigines recognize that what happens in dreamtime has a connection to what happens in waking life. The clan sits with the two parties in a place of unconditional, nonjudgmental love. The power of that presence provides the spiritual field for healing to take place, creating harmony in the group. They recognize the individual's place within the group: If someone is experiencing discomfort, it affects them all.

'Likewise, among the Hopi, when the elders were no longer physically able to work the harvest, their job became sitting together and flowing compassion and Divine Presence to the harvesters, the mothers, the small ones, and the ones yet to come. They were creating the vibration of Divine Love. This is Divine Acceptance – not resigning one's self, but flowing love to what is.'

This is Divine Acceptance – flowing love to what is.

Any time you use **Presence Practice** *to assist in clearing a particular judgment or feeling about another person, enter the* **Well** *and use the five steps to send love and compassion to them, until the painful feelings dissolve. Without expectation, observe the improvement in the relationship.*

'We invite ye to take one last look in the pool.' The ferryman winks, tips his captain's cap, and dissolves once more.

We lean closer to see what is there. The pool has become infinite in its scope, containing a vision of the totality of the Isle of Is, the Ocean of Being, the Universe, galaxies of stars, and all creation.

As we place the aquamarine back into the water, the gem begins to glow. Suddenly, a beam of light radiates from the stone and flows into our heart, where it illuminates our Inner Body, then spreads to create an exterior glow.

Our reflection fills us with awe. It is the Light being we saw in the Pool of (Ac)Knowledge. 'This is Divinity,' we think, understanding and welcoming what we have always been – Divine Light. We have come home to the brilliance.

From the facet of the stone we have seen our own image. It is compassion made manifest in the form of light.

11 | *The Stream of Consciousness*

The end is found in the beginning.
Once ye enter the Gate of Gratitude,
ye also enter the Stream.

Is-is waits for us in the pine tree that overhangs the falls. 'Hello, friend,' she crackles, spreading her wings in a regal gesture.

'Hello, Is-is!' We wave, happy to see her.

'And were the Cascades Divine?' she asks as we approach.

'Utterly Divine!'

'It's time to continue your travels,' she says. 'The Cascades flow into the Stream of Consciousness, which carries the consciousness of Divinity everywhere you go. You will follow the stream as it traverses the island.' The raven points downstream with her wing. 'It is your connection to the realm of Being. You see, the stream flows all the way to shore, where it merges with the Ocean of Being.'

Not far away is a trailhead and a roughly carved sign that reads: **Gently Down the Stream.**

'Will we need our map and keys?' we ask.

She tosses her ebony head. 'They were necessary when you first arrived.

Now you can use your intuition and the other gifts that the island has brought to your awareness.'

We smile. 'Sounds like graduation time!'

'It is true that you will be going home soon. The Stream will help you bring all your experiences together.'

The thought of leaving the island brings a pang of sadness. We wonder what it will be like to go home, back to our lives in the city. How much of this experience will we be able to take with us?

As always, Is-is knows our thoughts. 'Let me tell you about the Stream.' She nods toward the clear flowing water. 'The Stream of Consciousness is what connects everything – all the places and experiences on the island; all time; all space. Its banks touch the different aspects of conscious awareness – waking, sleeping, dreaming. It is a cosmic interlink that unifies everything.

The Stream is what connects everything: all time, all space.

'The Stream of Consciousness is you before you were born, you now, and you after you leave this body. It unifies space – here, there, and everywhere. It is the field or stream that connects the many different perceptions of Divinity – unconsciousness, awareness, and cosmic awareness. Your experiences in Is are always with you, in your own personal stream of consciousness. They are always in your quiver.'

We try to grasp this concept, which seems huge to us.

Is-is looks at us intently. 'It is the Stream of Consciousness that has helped you see the unification of all things. And on this next aspect of your journey, it will help you see even more.'

'Will it help us understand itself?' This seems a silly question, but we wish to understand this from a place of knowing.

'Oh, yes,' says Is-is. 'What you wish to know will be revealed to you.' She drops from the branch and lands on the grass in front of us. 'The earth is cool and the grass silky. We suggest that you take off your shoes and connect with your Earth Mother.' Is-is lifts one leg, displaying her bare foot.

We sit to take off our shoes, then tie them together in order to carry them over our shoulder. 'Goodbye, Is-is. Will we see you again?'

'Yes, you will. In the most unexpected places.' The raven dips her head, acknowledging us as Divine, then spreads her wings and, with a loud flapping, beats her large black wings until she vanishes into the forest canopy above.

Standing, we brush off our clothes and pause to feel the warmth and openness in our heart center as gratitude wells up inside us. It seems that we have known Is-is before, and we decide to tell our friends back home about meeting the Goddess Isis. With this thought, we hear a distant 'Caw-kra!' and know that she is affirming our sense that we have indeed known each other for a long time – an eternity, perhaps.

The path beckons. Glancing ahead, we see that someone has lined the path with small stones, and, at intervals, cairns of five stones each have been stacked by previous travelers. Usually left as markers for those who follow or to designate sacred spots, these cairns seem more playful – especially, as they are just a short distance apart. They also seem familiar. We have a brief recollection that, as a small child, we made these stacks when our mother told us what cairns were.

It is an odd sensation – a déjà vu. How could we have been here before? And yet in our mind's eye we see our child self running merrily about, collecting the flat stones and stacking them, as an offering to the deities who live in these parts.

Merrily. It's one of the words to the children's song. *Row row row your boat, gently down the stream.* As we set out down the trail, we find ourselves humming the tune. What are the rest of the lyrics? *Merrily merrily merrily merrily, life is but a dream.* It is a song about letting go into the flow of life! We hadn't thought about the lyrics when we sang it as a child. Now we know that when we are not so attached to the past or worried about the future, life becomes a dream, and more than that, it is the reality of Divinity itself. Even this momentary glance at our past has a quality of ease about it.

Ahead of us the grasses part and tiny wings flicker as small beings flit into our view, then flit briefly out of sight once more. We hear giggling, just as we thought we did early on our trip, but this time we know we are not imagining things. One winged being in a gossamer gown flies up from the grass and waves in our direction. Delighted, we smile and wave back.

We walk slowly in our bare feet, which heightens our senses. Heel and toes, heel and toes landing on the cool damp earth – a walking meditation. Doves coo in the limbs above, warblers whistle to one another in the undergrowth, and the stream murmurs over rocks, fallen twigs, and leaves.

Is-is called the ground beneath our feet our Earth Mother. But who, or what, is Mother Earth? Is she akin to Divine Mother, to our own flesh-and-blood mother, or to the other mothers we've encountered in meditation along the way? A knowing comes to us that she is all of these, a personification of all Divine mothers.

Beside us, the stream's murmurs increase. We pause to watch as it ripples around rocks and through crevices. 'Mother Earth,' it seems to be saying. 'I am Mother Earth.'

'Our Earth Mother?' we ask silently.

'Yes,' says the Stream. 'I am she, that feminine quality of creation that shows up in a myriad of ways – as your biological mother, your ancestral grandmothers, and all other Divine mothers, including the one who appeared to you in the forest. All mothers are connected to that Divine feminine aspect of creation. Our intention is to be with you at every step to nurture and support and unveil the truth of creation, as well as the essential truths that manifested creation. That is what a mother is.'

All mothers are connected to the Divine feminine aspect of creation.

If Mother Earth is *our* Earth Mother, then a personal relationship with her must be possible. Why hadn't we thought of that before? Looking around, a feeling of love and connection comes over us.

The Stream continues, 'Mother Earth has many aspects: trees, rocks, sand, soil, clay, mountains, pools, streams. She is the physical world that surrounds, nourishes, and protects you. Sit. Your Mother will tell you a story. A true story of how Mother Earth flows in the creation of lives of other individuals.'

We sit on a rock near the stream, placing our shoes and quiver beside us.

'Close your eyes,' says the Stream, 'the better to see the story.'

As we do, an image comes to us of a man – a holy man – sitting on a river bank, and the story unfolds.

A young swami in modern India is sitting beside a river in a deep state of meditation. He has gone into meditation questioning where he is to apply his knowledge – what Divine purpose is he here for?

He has been meditating for several hours and is in such a deep state of peace and joy that he does not fully realize that the river has begun to increase in flow. Torrential rain has been falling upstream and has swelled the river banks until the river has begun to rush headlong, flowing toward the Bay of Bengal, many kilometers away.

As the swami meditates, he sways to the rhythm of the river's currents. Before he realizes it, his body sways too close to the river, and he falls in.

The river is surging headlong over rocks, and the swami, surprised, tries to swim ashore. But the more he attempts to reach the bank, the more he loses ground. No matter how hard he swims, he cannot even gain hold of the rocks. Indeed, the river is taking him further and further away from where he had been sitting, to foreign shores further south.

Suddenly he hears a voice saying, 'Let go. Relax. Go with the flow of the river.' It seems to be the voice of God or Spirit, or perhaps Mother Earth.

At this, he turns onto his back and allows the river to take him downstream wrapped in its embrace. For a very long time he floats like this, giving himself up to the currents of the river and trusting Spirit to take care of him.

It has grown dark when at last he finds himself washing onto one of the banks. The river is quieter now, and it carries him easily into some rushes.

The swami climbs out of the river and wrings the water out of his robe. He walks up the bank to find a gathering of devotees, who bow down before him, as they know him to be an answer to their prayers, fulfilling a prophecy that a new swami would come to replace the one who has recently died. They have been waiting for their teacher to show up.

The young swami accepts this calling, for he, too, knows it to be an answer to his prayers. He sits with them that evening and speaks to them about the infinite power of Divinity and the importance of trust.

Listening to the story has put our mind in a dreamy, peaceful state. The Stream has become quieter, too, its murmurs a sweet whisper.

We open our eyes. 'The swami listened, didn't he?'

'It is an example of Divinity – of the nature of reality and how it all is. The swami asked to know his purpose from a place of inner peace, which is the most powerful way to manifest one's life. Likewise, from a place of seeking inner peace, the people asked for their teacher to come. Nature – Mother Earth – God – Spirit – responded by creating the rains and the increase in river flow, in order to deliver the swami to the people at just the right moment.'

'A synchronicity,' we exclaim, 'of the grandest kind.'

'Indeed, it is Spirit working in the world to manifest the highest good. When you recognize yourself as Divine, Divinity shows up everywhere. Everything becomes Divine, and you are connected to everything. More comes to you, and on a grander scale, as a result of your increased awareness and unveiled consciousness.'

'In the story, this happened because the swami and the people were in touch with Divinity, didn't it?'

The Stream murmurs assent. 'Take this to heart. Your presence in the world will show up differently when you return to your hometown. You will be operating from a sense of Divine purpose.'

We close our eyes and ask Spirit to help us take this in. It is an awesome thought.

When you recognize yourself as Divine, Divinity shows up everywhere.

A Stream of Travelers

Knowing it is time to continue our journey, we thank the Stream and set off once more. We sense that there will be other stops along the way. Thoughts of our Divine purpose and what that might be pass through our mind, yet we feel very present with our movements and our surroundings.

Before long we find ourselves at a small knoll above the stream. The views of the island are wide, and the sky is clear except for large puffs of clouds forming behind the mountains. To our delight we can see Mount Metaphor across a lush valley, its peak unmistakable in the late morning sun. Further down the mountain is the entrance to the gnomes' cave, and some distance away is a waterfall. We look closely: indeed, it is the Cascades of Compassion. From this distance, these landmarks appear as normal elements of Nature, but we know their magical qualities.

Something seems to be moving atop Mount Metaphor, and we squint to make out what it is. We realize it is a person walking around a rock, holding something under their arm – a book. Another traveler! We can see the images forming in their thoughts. Such an interesting metaphor they have come with! We can perceive the glorious experience they are having, and the growth in understanding. We glance down the slope. Sure enough, on the trail below, the gnomes are heading toward their cave. We would know those red chapeaus anywhere!

It is a wonderful thought, that others are also on the Isle of Is – just behind us and, no doubt, ahead of us as well. The island is indeed an organic place, and the individuals who come here are a part of that organic, undulating process of Divinity. It's just the Is-ness of the island. Our perception is that this traveler could have been before us, or after us. We feel we are looking at a cosmic videotape that we could fast-forward or rewind. It is all happening synchronistically, outside of time.

If the traveler is indeed behind us, she will follow the gnomes to their cave, where she will mine for her old metaphor. Later she will reach into the pool at the Vein of God to retrieve her personal gemstone, and still later sit behind the gushing waterfall to contemplate compassion and devotion.

We think of how these aspects of the island fit together for us – our old metaphor, *Life is Sisyphus Pushing a Boulder Uphill;* the new metaphor, *Life is an Ocean of Being;* and the understanding that we are to flow compassion and devotion to ourselves. The old metaphor certainly made it difficult to do so – we were too caught up in trying to keep that boulder from rolling over us! Although, heaven knows, we needed compassion.

As Being, we can flow compassion infinitely to the world.

Life is an Ocean of Being means that everything is Being, including us. When our mind tells us that we have done something wrong or that we are unworthy, we can remember the metaphor – that we are Being – and flow compassion toward our mind and ego. As Being, we are infinite and can flow compassion infinitely to the world. Loving ourselves comes first, because if we are caught up in judging ourselves, then it is hard to remember that we are Divine, and difficult to flow love toward others.

*Take a few moments to consider the old metaphor, the new metaphor, and what you have learned about compassion and devotion. Do you have any new understandings about how these fit together for you personally? If it is helpful, pick up your **Wand** and free-write about this for a few minutes.*

We peer again at the small figure of the traveler atop Mount Metaphor.

A feeling of compassion comes over us – for ourselves and for all island travelers.

We see how perfect it is that we decided to come to the Isle of Is, and how blessed we are to have these experiences. It would be fun to meet other travelers and share about our journey and our being. Perhaps this will be the case. Anna awaits us back home, and we are deeply grateful that this is so.

The Body Speaks

Glancing ahead, we see that the trail leaves the knoll and circles back to the stream. We set out once more, humming a happy tune. After meandering close to the bank for a while, we are soon in the midst of deep forest, with crickets, frogs, and parrots calling all around us. In the shade of dense overhanging branches, it is humid and cool. Joined by many rivulets as it flows downhill, the stream has become wider; its murmurs have become gurgling.

Before long, we arrive at a place where the trail crosses the stream. A row of stepping stones allows one to ford to the other side, and the trail picks up on the opposite bank. In fact, the path is wet there, as though someone has recently crossed ahead of us. On our side of the stream is a sign with arrows pointing to the left and right, but no words. We know we are to cross the stream and wonder what the sign signifies.

To our left is forest similar to what we have been passing through. We study the trees for what it is we are to notice. Then we spy a small opening among the trees, at a perfect height for peering through. We draw close. Beyond the opening is a clearing where something black and shiny reflects the sun. At first we cannot make out what it is, then we notice words carved above it: fone home. It is the phone on the tree where Divine Mother called us! The tree in the Forest of Forgetfulness! Her voice wafts on the breeze . . . *You are never far from Is-ness* . . . and we hear the sound of the phone ringing within our heart. Our experiences since leaving the Forest have given us a deeper understanding of the truth of these words – and the Stream is affirming it every step of the way. Indeed, all of our knowings are close at hand.

We hear the sound of the phone ringing within our heart.

Feeling the energy of Divine Mother's presence, we return to the stream and, stone by stone, step across. On the other side is more forest, but the trees are wider apart. Suddenly we realize that briars surround the trees, and we know that there is another old tree there, in the Briar of Beliefs. We remember fondly our night snuggled among the tree's roots and the feeling of being cared for by a tree. Just then, we catch sight of the upper branches of the old tree, which sways ever-so-slightly at our notice.

We have come a long way since the Briar and the Forest. Our old beliefs have become less tangled and have lessened their hold on our mind. The new metaphor has helped a great deal by giving us a new image for life and a new sense of reality. The new metaphor has also revealed the old beliefs for what they truly were . . . limiting.

As for remembering who and what we are, we find it is becoming easier and easier. Once we return to our home town, if we should slip and forget, we can always enter the Well or pick up our Wand. And Divine Mother is just a phone call away.

Encountering the Forest and the Briar again, makes us wonder if there is anything else we wish to let go of – anything within the body, the emotions, or our beliefs that we might see from a greater place of openness and clarity. We decide to ask the Stream.

As we crouch to sit on the bank after the long downhill walk, we become aware that our knees are throbbing – remnants of an old injury, from a fall we took as a child. We have the thought that it will feel good to immerse our knees in the cool stream.

As we wade into the water, Mother Earth speaks again through the Stream. 'You have experienced Spirit through the birds, trees, bushes, flowers, mountains, caves, and pools – all the crevices and orifices of my body, the Earth. Just so with the different parts of your body. All the parts are sacred.'

The appropriateness of the message astonishes us, and we reach down to caress our knees.

The body that you inhabit is a creation of Divine Presence.

'The body that you inhabit is a manifestation, a creation of Divine Presence. The body is a portal or doorway that leads to a deeper experience of Presence. By being *in* the body – bringing your awareness fully into the body – you can strengthen being in a state of Presence. This helps dispel the old metaphor.'

'Being in the body?' we ask, somewhat puzzled. 'What does the body have to do with it?'

'Just now, your knees are speaking to you, are they not?' The Stream gently massages our knees with its currents. 'By honoring whatever aspect of the body gives you a signal – in this case, your knees – you have the opportunity to be focused in the Present.'

Instinctively we take a deep breath, relax into the body, and feel the sensations.

'Yes, just like that,' says the Stream. 'It is worthy to go to the source of the sensation. This is a place where your energy is held. Take your attention there and allow the sensation to be released. Go there to recapture the energy that is rightfully yourself.'

Bring your awareness to the body and begin **Presence Practice**. *Take a few moments with each element:*
> *Breathe.*
> *Relax into the body.*
> *Feel the sensations.*
> *Notice the sensations.*
> *Send feelings of love to the sensations and to the body.*

CD Track 5: Presence Practice

You can use this practice when you feel caught up in emotion or bodily discomfort; you can also use it anytime, anywhere. Its purpose is to bring you into a state of Presence, where feelings of well-being, peace, and joy are your constant companions. By entering **Presence Practice** *often, you will find a qualitative change in your moment-to-moment experience of life.*

The throbbing has ceased, and we are grateful to the Stream, which courses and spills around us.

'Often, emotions, thoughts, and beliefs linger in the body and speak to us through the body,' says the Stream. 'If we honor the sensations by being present with them, rather than numbing them out by various means, we allow not only the sensations, but also the emotions, thoughts, and beliefs to be released. When painful feelings come up, give them your full Presence. Shine the light of your Presence on them – because you are the light. Being with the body is an important aspect of being in Is. It is a major trick of the ego to deny the body's needs.'

'Why would the ego do that?' we ask.

'There are two major reasons. First, the ego is invested in appearances. If the ego thinks that going to bed early, abstaining from alcohol, or not eating dessert, would seem strange to someone else, the ego wishes to keep you from following the body's directives. It wishes to keep your approval rating high.

'The second reason has to do with your identification with the body – thinking that the body is *you*. By calling the body *my* body, we identify it with the ego, which attaches us to the thoughts and feelings of how other people have perceived this body.'

'Others such as . . . ?'

'Parents, teachers, physicians, romantic partners, and society in general. Society's concepts of how the body should look, which you see in magazines and on television, invade your ego and make your ego think this body is imperfect. The ego is committed to gaining society's and others' approval. If cosmetic surgery or becoming Mr Muscle Man would cause others to approve – regardless of the effect on the body – then the ego will push you toward the appearance of perfection.'

The Stream's words hit home, as we have found ourselves drinking beer with Jane to keep her company, and putting off exercise in favor of watching the evening news, which we think makes us a lively conversationalist at work. Both of these choices have negative consequences for the body – and the mind.

The Stream continues. 'Our life in society is a collection of interactions with others' egos, each of them in a place of judgment. Calling it *my* body puts us in a place of judgment, of identification with others' egos and comparing it with their images and ideals.'

'What should we call it, then, if not *our* body?'

'Call it *the* body, which does not belong to the ego or mind. It is *the* body that you are inhabiting for a while.'

As you do **Presence Practice** *with the body's sensations, remind yourself that it is not your pain or your body – but* **the** *pain and* **the** *body. This discomfort and this body are truly temporary. 'I am not the pain. I am a Divine being.'*

Presence Practice *helps you to release discomfort, to develop your Presence, and to stay in the Present. It will assist you in avoiding escapism through various means – drugs, alcohol, overwork, overeating, and more.*

It's true. There are times when we have ignored the body's messages and escaped into alcohol, television, and overwork.

'Perhaps it will be easier to look at how this has happened to others,' says the Stream, and an image of our friend Zoe comes to mind.

Zoe became ill after many years of serving food to indigent people in soup kitchens. Years earlier, she had moved into a house in a rundown neighborhood, and within a year the city built an incinerator nearby. Over time the fumes and gases increased, exposing Zoe to airborne toxins. Faulty air conditioning led to excess mold in her basement, and damaged plumbing leaked sewage into the lower level of the house as well. Zoe continued to live in the house because it was easy to get to the soup kitchens. For reasons of convenience and because Zoe felt others' needs were more important than her own, she was not attentive to herself. Asthma, arthritis, even a long bout of pneumonia did not rouse Zoe's concern. She was shocked when she developed leukemia – her body's desperate cry for her attention. Zoe then began a regimen of vitamins, chemotherapy, and exercise, but she did not move out of the house, and the leukemia lingered in her body's cells.

'It is an unfortunate situation,' says the Stream, 'but such examples abound. In your own family, for example, your cousin Henry had a heart attack, even though he had meditated for 15 years. He took care of the mind, but not the body. No amount of meditating can offset the effect of eating a rib-eye steak and a carton of ice cream every evening.'

It is a sober reminder for us as well. Henry was surprised by the heart attack, but others who knew him were not. He weighed over 250 pounds at the time his heart gave out.

'And how about yourself?' asks the Stream. 'Might you, too, listen better to the body?'

Might you, too, listen better to the body?

'Yes, we think so.' We leave the stream bed and seat ourselves on a rock, taking out our Wand and writing pad.

*With your **Wand**, free-write your answer to the question, 'How might I listen better to the body?' What messages does the body give you about sleep, stress, meditation, drinking water, alcohol, smoking cigarettes, exercise, diet, and more? How well do you listen to these messages? Write for at least 15 minutes.*

When you have finished writing, choose one of these messages that you will listen to and honor, beginning today. Write this on a slip of paper and post it where you will see it: 'I will _____ each day, to honor my Self as Divine.'

As we write, we realize that the body gives us many messages! Messages about our posture and which chairs to sit in. Messages about how warmly to dress and the kind of shoes to put on our feet. Some messages are specific to a particular time and place: "Drink another glass of water before you go on this walk." Other messages are generic and hold true over time: "Go to bed by 10:00 pm so that you will feel bright and alert each morning."

We decide that we will write *two* things and post them when we return to our home town – going to bed by 10:00 pm, and choosing not to drink alcohol with Jane when she requests it. When we have finished writing, we close our quiver.

The body knows itself as Divine.

The Stream speaks. 'The body knows itself as Divine, but the ego keeps us from perceiving this truth. All the body's messages are designed to help us return to the knowledge that the body is a Divine creation.

'In its present state, the body will not last for eternity. It exists in time and space, but its purpose is to help you know and understand your limitlessness. Existing in the physical realm, it points you toward the realm of infinite Divinity.'

We reflect on these words, understanding that honoring the body's wisdom will help us remember we are Divine. Likewise, by remembering that we are Divine, we will wish to honor the body even more.

Immersion Excursion

We thank the Stream and return to the trail, which soon leads to a bamboo footbridge. Curious. It is the same bridge we crossed en route from the Briar of Beliefs to the Ever-Present, with its abundance of jingling bellflowers. Once on the opposite bank, however, we notice that the sign has been changed. It no longer points straight ahead toward the meadow, but rather, to the right, downstream – further evidence of the perfection that awaits us at every juncture as we follow the Stream.

Here we re-enter the forest, where sunlight filters through the branches, dappling our path. A breeze whispers in the leaves, one of Mother Earth's most calming voices.

We had not been aware of our knees bothering us earlier in the day, but now we notice the difference. The walk is easier when our knees are not throbbing. We express gratitude for the sensations in our knees, which led us to valuable new understandings. Perhaps it is the nature of all pains and diseases to bring us additional information and wisdom. Now as we walk, we breathe, relax, and feel, noticing how the sensations in the knees have changed.

In time, the path leads to an overlook above the stream. We climb slowly, maintaining an even pace. Once on top, we gaze out across a meadow. It is the meadow of the Ever-Present, where notes waft on the breeze. Buda and the 'Hood are singing their *sangha,* perhaps for another traveler.

Beyond the meadow is a valley, and on the far side of the valley, a ridge that leads to a cliff high above the ocean, where three ancient stones stand as sentry for the Isle of Is. It is this cliff where the rock guided us to feel its vibrations and experience our own energy. And, of course, beyond the cliff is the Ocean of Being. From our observation point we can see whitecaps rolling over the reef amid a palette of turquoise blues and greens.

We think of how the Ever-Present, the Waves of Energy, and the Ocean of Being are all interconnected as one Presence, one Being-ness. Our introduction to each place came from the creatures of Mother Nature – bugs and butterflies, a large flat rock, and an opalescent white fish. The stream, the raven, the spider, the mushroom – all have been our teachers – along with the ferryman, Divine Mother, and the gnomes, of course. Closing our eyes, we thank Mother Earth and all her creatures for their continuing assistance. We make a mental note that we can take the island home with us by continuing to immerse ourselves in Nature, where all beings live in the Ever-Present.

The word 'immerse' stays in our thoughts, as we have a sudden desire to immerse ourselves in the stream. Indeed, a few yards beyond where we stand, the path winds down to the stream. This synchronicity – our thought, and the path leading to the stream – is evidence of our state of Presence. We follow a series of short switchbacks until we reach the water's edge. Beside the stream is a water hole bounded on all sides by rocks, a perfect place for a dip.

We dive into the clear, deep water. It is cool and fresh, which helps in the magnetic frequencies about us, enhancing the new metaphor even further. It feels as though we have entered the new metaphor totally, in a kind of cleansing or baptism. This experience recalls Celtic and Egyptian mystery schools that used cool water as a means of solidifying the spiritual aspirant's intent. As well, the native peoples of the Americas and New Zealand – Hopi, Aztec, Inca, Maori – for centuries have used water in acts of healing and purification. In this state of purity, we feel the sun's rays entering the water and flowing through us, as though we are filled with particles of Divine energy.

Easing ourselves onto a rock, we sit in the sun and begin the Meditation in the Ever-Present, an immersion in light and silence.

> **Meditation in the Ever-Present:** *Close your eyes and bring your awareness to the breath. Set aside any concerns or thoughts of past and future.*
>
> *Visualize and feel light pouring down. Visualize light entering the body on the breath, filling the body, and enlivening every cell.*
>
> *Remain in silence for 30 minutes. If the mind drifts and pulls you out of the feeling of Divine Presence, bring the mind back to the sensations of light in the body.*

We open our eyes and glance around at the water hole, the stream, the lookout point. Everything seems to be light: light bouncing in the water, light beaming broadly in the sky, light shimmering on the hillside above. As we step onto the bank, the white fish swims by, all glitter and shine. It jumps in the water, waving its fin in recognition of our being in the Stream of Consciousness, constantly flowing into the Ocean of Being.

It's Elemental

We gaze downstream, where water flows toward the sea. We know we will carry our immersion experience with us, wherever our path leads, wherever we need to go. Indeed, the path appears wherever we place our feet. The experience has a quality we have not known before, as though each moment is materializing just for us.

The trail has begun its descent toward the beach, zigzagging alongside the stream, which continues to grow in magnitude as it nears the Ocean of

Being. In places, the stream gushes over rocks and spills over ledges. It is as though an orchestra, finally tuned up, is playing vibrato, full force. We are thrilled by the sensation of the vibrations created by the tumbling water. It has become more than a stream, more than itself. It has become a river of consciousness, a river of life.

We come to a configuration of rocks in the stream that looks like a chair with a back, seat, and armrests. Water flows over the back, spilling onto the seat. We wish to sit there and take in the view, but to reach it, we must cross the stream. The water is deep here, and gushing. We stand on the bank, gazing across. Will we muster the courage to enter the stream at this point?

Then we hear a voice: 'Trust. Relax. You *are* the flow.' We sense that it is the voice of the young swami, now older and more mature.

*Trust. Relax.
You are the flow.*

Taking a deep breath, we step out over the water. To our astonishment, a lotus pad appears where once there was none. It floats to us, we step on it, and it glides over the water, carrying us across. We feel so much in unity with Divinity that everything operates in our favor.

At the configuration of rocks, we step off the lotus pad and ease into the chair, leaning back fully so that the water flows over us. It is an auspicious place, with splendid views over aspects of the island and the Ocean of Being. We sense that this is a throne where kings and queens of old – or perhaps elemental forces of sprites and devas – once sat.

A slight noise behind us causes us to turn. More than half a dozen fairies in gossamer gowns and jeweled headdresses are circling from behind. Their entrance is magical, their physical selves materializing so that we might see them. A diffused light like moonshine emanates from their translucent forms.

'And who might you be?' we ask, delighted.

'Ceres, Papatuanuku, Gyffes, Haumea, Dakuwangga, Devi, and Angus Mac Og,' say seven tiny voices. 'People of peace.'

Emeralds, rubies, and blue sapphires sparkle on their gowns. Upon closer examination we see that one sports a lion's mane; another, celestial markings in the form of a tattoo. Still others carry a magic wand, a harp, and a bundle of golden grain.

'We see from your apparel that you are kings and queens.'

The fairies bow in unison, tipping their crowns and headdresses in our direction.

'And you as well,' says the one called Gyffes, his voice bright and tinkly. 'It is your birthright. It is *everybody's* birthright.'

'We have seen you along the way,' we say, 'at the Gate of Gratitude and along the stream. It is an honor to receive your visit.'

Inside Devi's uterus is an orb that reflects the Universe. Her right hand carries joy and pain; her left hand, life and death. 'We have looked after you, making sure you take the right turns.' As she speaks, the orb's image transmutes into the Gate of Gratitude, and we see ourselves heading down the trail to the Pool of (Ac)Knowledge.

'We once sat on this throne,' says Dakuwangga, clothed in a shark's body. He waves his fin to create tiny bubbles that waft on the breeze and settle on our skin. 'It is where Divinity sits.'

Others chime in. 'It is also where we see Divinity outside us.'

'And in everything.'

Haumea, in a grass skirt and headdress of seven serpents, gestures toward the Ocean of Being in the distance. As she does, the serpents move their heads, smiling. 'And what do you see before you?'

In a sudden gust of wind, the trees below us part, exposing the Pool of (Ac)Knowledge with its surrounding rock wall. Just as quickly, the wind moves on, parting again to reveal an arch covered in blossoms – the Gate of Gratitude.

'You have embraced the lessons of the island well – gratitude and acknowledging synchronicities,' says Ceres in her cornucopia headdress. 'You have come a long way since entering that sacred gate.'

'The experiences have been wondrous.' we say. 'Visits to the Well, feeling energy, writing with our Wand, and all the beings who have helped us. These have led us to a constant state of gratitude. Situations we once found difficult to be grateful for – physical discomfort, Mother's fearfulness, Grandma's drinking, even the prospect of Grandpa's death – we can now embrace with gratitude.'

The meditations flash before us – the Ever-Present and the Divine Personalities. These have revealed the gratitude inside us that has always been there. We will take these precious experiences home with us.

'The essence of the meditations is in the silence. The magic is in the silence,' says Haumea, who lifts a magic stick to bless us. As she does so, papaya trees nearby burst into fruit. 'We suggest that you enter the Well twice a day for half an hour each time. Doing it twice will give you four times the benefit.'

'Or more,' says Angus Mac Og, flicking his fingers, which erupt into many-colored feathers. 'Our advice is simple: Meditate twice a day, and use Presence Practice to bring you into Divine Presence in every moment.'

He blows us a kiss, which transforms into a parrotfinch with a slip of paper in its beak. The bird drops the paper into our hands. It says, *'Love Is.'*

'Being in the Well,' says Angus, 'is the only time most humans immerse themselves in uninterrupted silence. It is truly an immersion experience. Living calmly and peacefully is not the same thing as permeating one's being with silence. Do not let your mind convince you of that.'

The other fairies nod in agreement.

Angus flutters his wings almost imperceptibly. 'It is my responsibility to flutter in humans' ears when they listen to their minds on such topics. Humans say, 'I meditate all the time,' meaning that they are generally at peace with their environment, yet their life's activity contains much distress. Their mind and their metaphor trick them into thinking otherwise. It is not the same as entering the Well. If they would enter the Well twice a day for one month, their lives would be vastly different!'

'In time, the drama of their lives would disappear,' says Devi. Her hands frame the orb in her abdomen, which is distorted in appearance. As we watch, the orb becomes crystalline clear.

'As for particular meditations,' says Papatuanuku, resplendent in her yellow and purple gown with its blue gems and ribbons, 'the Meditation in the Ever-Present brings health, healing, and great awareness of the body. Do it as you fall asleep, or if you are sick or have a chronic physical situation.'

Gyffes raises a scepter decorated with mother-of-pearl, which reflects the brilliance of all the royal fairy folk. 'Meditate with the Divine Personalities daily, for they will enable you to bring such Divine Presence into your life . . . ah!' He waves his tiny hand in front of our face, motioning us to close our eyes.

Enter the **Meditation with Divine Personalities**. *Close your eyes and* *enter the silence of the Well. Call forth Mother Earth, Is-is, the white fish, or other Divine personalities of the Isle of Is. Feel the Divine Presence of each. Remain in silence for 30 minutes or longer.*

We become aware that this was the deepest meditation yet. A feeling of expansiveness, and yet a sense of serenity pervades our being as though we had traveled to the bottom of the ocean.

As our awareness begins to shift to the environment around us, we hear the rumble of waves and the lapping of water on the beach. Curious, we slowly open our eyes.

Indeed, we are seated on the beach, and in our hand is the last key.

12 | *Tides of Truth*

Ye Are That.

The Vedas

On the beach to our right is a gleaming structure made of sand. The sun glints on it so that we cannot make out what it is. Three children are playing there, and we start to call out to them.

But no, it is the gnomes in brightly colored, old-fashioned bathing suits – paisley, flowered, and plaid – plastic buckets in tow. Sand pours from their shovels. Paisley makes an arc with his arm and hand, behind which a rainbow forms that points to the structure. Now we see it – a large, elaborate sand castle. It looks like one we constructed as a child, a project that elicited much glee.

As we venture down the beach to investigate, the gnomes turn away from the beach and disappear into the forest. We stop short at the castle. It is a grand structure with turrets and cupolas, arched doorways, and passages curving this way and that. The finishing touches are delightful: mother-of-pearl windows, pebble walkways, and tiny red flags fluttering atop the turrets. We find ourselves interested in making more ornamental touches and reach for small pink and blue shells scattered on the beach in order to decorate the walls.

We are about to press the shells into the outer walls when a cloud drifts overhead, creating a dark cast over the castle. Around us, the beach is still bright in the sun; only the castle is in shade. As we puzzle about this, we notice that the tide is coming in. One, two, three waves run toward us, then fall back. The next wave, more forceful than the others, rushes up the beach and crashes over the castle, obliterating it.

'Oh, my!' We are surprised and a bit disappointed. The castle in all its grandeur has been washed away. In its place is a melting heap of sand, pebbles, shells, and half a dozen red flags.

We stand, hands on our hips. 'Now what?' we say out loud, wondering what could be the meaning of this. After all, the gnomes built this castle! Why would this structure, so spendidly constructed, fall away?

'The castle was an illusion, like life is an illusion,' a deep voice rumbles above us. We look up at the cloud floating above our head. 'It might be fun, and it might be grand, but it is not real,' says the cloud. 'It's an artificial real, washed away by the Ocean of Being and the Tides of Truth.'

Illusion. Reality. Artificial real. Isn't life reality?

'What's real is the Divinity within everything,' continues the cloud. 'This is what abides over time. This is what is.'

What's real is the Divinity within everything.

'Okay, yes, we know that. We have learned this in our travels on the island. But isn't life real? How confusing if it's not!' We realize there is a look of consternation on our face.

'You have known yourself as a limited being, an ego, a self. What you are in reality is the Self – the Cosmic Self,' says the cloud. 'Just as I am not merely a cloud. The voice coming through me is the Cosmic Self as well.'

We shake our head. 'Divinity we understand, but not Cosmic Self.'

The cloud hovers between us and the sun, shading our eyes. 'I am that voice of Truth you have been communicating with all along – and I am all the other characters you have encountered on the island as well. I am the Divine that communicates through all creation. You, too, are That.'

'But we live in this life. You called this life an illusion.'

'Indeed, that is how it is. And as long as you know that your life situation is an illusion, it is fine to be immersed in it. You can have fun, explore, enjoy

– add shells to the sand castle. But people get caught up in the illusion: two cars in the sand garage, spending time at their sand jobs, stashing money in the sand bank, counting the days until sand retirement. They get caught up and forget who it is that they really are.'

We know what the cloud is speaking about. Back home we saw this all around us. 'People try to keep up with the Johnsons and the Smiths,' we muse.

'And the Singhs and the Kumars. The Romeros and the Garcias.'

A cloud with a sense of humor! We laugh.

'Your life situation is not your life. It is a menagerie of the constructed relative world. Your ego is just grains of sand creating the illusion. The truth is that everything is Divine, and it's always there.'

'And what about Self – Cosmic Self?'

'On the island, Cosmic Self has been introducing your ego self to the Big Self in numerous creative ways – through characters and stories – gemstones and sand castles – cascades and pools.'

'And I am That? We are all the same thing?'

'In essence, yes.'

'But why does Self need the world, if it is already Divine?'

'Merely for its Divine play. As a means of Divinity being and acting in the world. The Big Self has been parading as all these other characters, as this Divine assistance. All you need do is come to the realization that you and All That Is are One.'

The Highest Choice

We look out to sea, in the direction of our life back home. We have experienced many wondrous things on the island. And we know that we can always revisit the Wand and the Well. But still we are concerned that the busy-ness of our everyday life will consume us and Divinity will elude us.

The tides have begun to wash over our feet on their incoming runs. Now a wave speaks. 'Things will be different when you return, not the way it once was. Even though you are leaving this island, which is the epitome of support and unfoldment, we shall be with you forever as you travel back to your previous realm.'

'You, the Cosmic Self, will be with us?' we ask.

'Yes. We are everywhere. There is no place that we are not present.'

As a youth we had read George MacDonald fairytales in which the princess received all manner of assistance. The stories provided solace to us as we embarked on adulthood. At one point, Grandmother gives the princess a silver thread to hold onto when she goes into the cave in search of truth. 'With this silver thread, you can always find your way home,' said the Grandmother.

'And Cosmic Self is my silver thread?' we ask the wave.

'Indeed. A silver thread that is present in every person, every building, every lamppost, every tree.'

We look around at the sunlight that stretches long upon the beach, at the tide pools where tiny crabs scurry to bury themselves in the sand. At our feet are shells, coins of the sea. Above us, clouds scuttle across an azure sky, while before us is the deep ocean blue, where the waves undulate, bringing Beingness to melt with the Island of Is in an endless cycle.

We realize that if we move by increments – slowing down, simplifying our life – we will move in synchronicity with Nature. In this way we will be in touch with Divinity, with the silence.

The tides speak. 'We tides are evidence of the movement of powerful forces. Our sister the Moon and our mother the Earth work in harmony, supporting life in a myriad of forms. Your life, too, is a tide, a movement within the physical realm, a wave upon the sea. All you need do is remember that the Ocean is your source – indeed, that the Ocean is you. Being human and having a choice, the highest choice is to acknowledge your Self as Divine. You can also do this by choosing teachers, friends, experiences, and teachings that recognize your Divinity.'

The highest choice is to acknowledge your Self as Divine.

We know that the tides have spoken an important truth.

Suddenly a stream of words and images fills our senses – a stream of consciousness.

'Dear one,' says a wave.

'Sweetness,' says another.

'Love incarnate,' says a third.

Stardust twinkles over the water, and Gyffes appears, his crown glimmering in the late afternoon light. 'Meditate with the Divine Personalities daily . . .' He holds up a wooden sign: '. . . for **The Treasure Lies Within**.' It is the sign we saw at the entrance of the gnomes' cave.

As Gyffes fades from view, Haumea materializes in her queenly finery, her wings fluttering, her wand sprinkling fairy dust. 'The magic is in the silence . . .' she whispers.

'. . . and the answers ye seek are inside ye.' The ferryman has come into view, his face shining in the clarity of the Pool of (Ac)Knowledge.

Under our gaze, the Pool gives way to the Ever-Present.

'Notice the silence and the space,' says Conscious Caterpillar, tilting her head as if to listen. 'These will take you to the Ever-Present any time you wish.'

Buda Bug reclines on a branch nearby, front legs clasped behind his head. He winks at us. 'This is Heaven, man.'

We smile, forever grateful, for it is through Nature's creatures that we have come to experience the Ever-Present wherever we go.

'When you recognize yourself as Divine, Divinity shows up everywhere,' murmurs Mother Earth in her character as the Stream.

The kindly old tree, sentinel of the Briar of Beliefs, leans beside the Stream. 'Divinity is your true identity,' he says.

These images fade, and our focus is drawn to the ocean itself, which speaks from its depths. 'Divinity is your true identity,' it echoes. 'Allow this to be the thought that you carry into your days and nights.'

We remember our new metaphor – Life Is an Ocean of Being – and the deep peace and joy that it brings.

Flowered Gnome rides on the waves, tipping his scarlet hat. 'Keep the words and images of the new metaphor in yer heart,' he says. And we touch our heart in response.

The image of Is-is floats before us – she who along with Divine Mother and the Stream of Consciousness taught us to honor feelings, sensations, and the body. 'The Divine You is great love and great power,' the black bird says. 'Flow love and compassion toward yourself. From there, it flows to the rest of the Universe.'

The Divine You is great love and great power.

The idea of this brings a feeling of softness to our Presence.

As the image of the raven fades, Mount Metaphor comes into view, emerging above the ocean's mist. Pages are turning in the Book of Life. When they stop, the words on the page reverberate inside us: 'The Divine You is meant to live in this place of Is as an expression of your Divinity.'

Yes, we know it deeply. We *can* live in this place of Is, regardless of where we travel.

The cosmic telephone rings. 'Remember,' says Divine Mother, 'you are never far from Is-ness.'

This cosmic moment, this connection with the infinite voices and images of Cosmic Self, brings a feeling of deep awe. The teachings have been many, yet the teaching is truly One.

'Is *is,*' we say.

13 | *The Constant Cosmos of Is*

Divine are ye inside and out,
And ye make holy whatever ye touch or are touched from.

Walt Whitman

The rowboat is coming in on the tide. We take the ring of keys from the quiver and place them on the sand for whoever comes after us, then wade into the water. We are surprised to see that the ferryman is not in the boat. Instead, three sailors are rowing with gusto, chanting 'Heave ho!' – The Volga Boat Song. It is the gnomes in sailor shirts, bow ties, and white hats. Their ties, of course, are plaid, paisley, and flowered.

'Ahoy!' calls Plaid

'Avast, ye matey!' calls Flowered.

'Welcome ye Self aboard!' says Paisley, extending a gnarled hand to help us into the small boat.

As we settle onto a bench, the gnomes begin rowing toward the Boat E. Satva, pulling the oars in one long sweep before lifting them out of the water and pulling again.

'We saw you at the sand castle!' we exclaim. 'You are just about every-where!'

'Aye,' says Plaid, grinning. 'The Ever-Present is.'

They groan and grunt as they maneuver the boat close to the ship. Once the rowboat is tied up, the gnomes give us a gentle push from behind, helping us up the ladder.

From the deck the ferryman reaches out and clasps our hand, which we gratefully accept. On his shoulder perches the raven.

'Is-is!' we say happily. 'We thought we might not see you again!'

'Your devoted friend,' the ferryman says to both of us at once, stroking the raven.

'Ever more,' she caws.

'Ever more,' we say, smiling.

As the sails unfurl, we make our way to the aft deck, where we can look back at the island. The sun is setting, its muted rays tingeing the trees and hills of Is with gold. Mount Metaphor rises above the hills and valleys, majestic and grand. It is a stunning sight, one we wish to keep in mind forever.

The island takes its place in the cosmos.

The ocean is calm, the journey smooth, and night comes gently. Above us the planets, stars, and galaxies of the Milky Way are diamond points in the infinite Cosmos of Is. The island takes its place in the cosmos – one Divine point among all the others.

In time, the ferryman comes to find us at the back of the ship. 'We'll be reaching your home town soon.' He points out the twinkling lights on the shore.

Indeed, it is beautiful – as beautiful as the sight we have just left behind, and as beautiful as the sight in the night sky above. Together we walk to the prow.

Instead of docking the ship, the ferryman anchors offshore, and we three climb into the rowboat – the ferryman, Is-is, and our Self – in order to row to the jetty. Our family and friends line the dock: Mother, Jane, Grandpa, Grandma, Auntie May, Luke, Anna, Samuel the mailman. They are waving at us, and we wave back. A feeling of tenderness suffuses our being.

Just as the ferryman eases the boat alongside the dock, the white fish leaps from the water, then dives into the Ocean of Being. We lean over for a closer look. As we follow its image, the surface clears and we catch a glimpse of our Self. We are wearing the captain's hat, and Is-is sits on our shoulder!

'What. . . ?' we stutter.

The ferryman hands us the oars. 'I'm off to sign up new recruits,' he says, climbing out of the boat. 'Got a book tour, and some meetings with devotees. Ye will have the joy of helping others to the island.'

We watch in astonishment as our family and friends climb into the boat, Grandma hiking her skirt up to her knees, displaying her ruby slippers; Grandpa, invigorated by the ocean air, dropping his cane on the dock before stepping down; Auntie May carrying a bouquet of tinkling bellflowers, which she hands to us, smiling sweetly. Mother wears a paisley blouse, flowered scarf, and plaid skirt – an outfit to make any gnome proud of their Divine Mother. Jane carries her guitar case, and Samuel has a quiver similar to the one the ferryman gave us. We catch Anna's eye, and she beams at us.

Everyone has found a seat, and we glance around the dock for the ferryman, now joined by two golden retrievers who prance joyfully around him.

'Ye know your job, don't ye?' the ferryman calls out to us, his face shining.

We nod. 'To help everyone get to Is!'

Glossary of Spiritual Terms

name of
boat
+
Boat of truth

awakening – the experience of living more and more in a state of peace, joy, and connection to everything, which is one's natural state. In the past, awakening has been discussed in terms of requiring lifetimes; now the possibility has presented itself that one can awaken by bringing one's awareness consistently to Divine Presence in a particular lifetime. It can even happen spontaneously.

Being – the underlying divine quality that exists within and without time and space; a primordial experience of one's Divinity that has no beginning and no end.

bodhisattva – one who has reached a certain state of enlightenment and has made the choice to remain in the cycle of life and death in order to help those who have not yet reached that state. The bodhisattva's role is to be an example, a teacher, and a presence.

buddhahood – the concept of acknowledging one's Divinity and living that.

consciousness – the level of one's ability to perceive one's self as Divine, and to understand the ratio between ego and absolute cosmic understanding, beyond the intellect. Being in a state of consciousness is more than just being awake. One can be completely aware of one's Divinity throughout various states of awareness – waking, dreaming, and deep sleep without dreaming.

Divine Presence – essentially the same as Being, but it is how Being expresses itself with characteristics. A human or other sentient being can experience the Divine Presence of air, space, trees, persons, all things.

Divinity – one's natural existence beyond creation. Divinity is everything's natural existence beyond creation.

ferryman – one who is capable of traveling from one side to the other.

The Field – another name for Being, generally spoken about in scientific terms such as energy, electromagnetic presence, photons, electrons, etc.

free writing – a writing process that involves a flow of words, feelings, thoughts, and images, where the writer does not plan or consciously construct what they are going to write.

integrity – the point at which one's consciousness enters the realm where one is able to comprehend Truth, per the work of David Hawkins.

karma – the law of natural consequences; cause and effect; the Golden Rule. In the belief system of karma, one carries the residuals of past deeds into their present life, makes amends, and benefits from "good" deeds. The cycle of birth and death is circumvented when the individual has atoned for all their past "evil" deeds. This is referred to as liberation – being liberated from the cycle of earthly birth and death.

metaphor – an image or figure of speech used to help understand something by defining it in terms of something else, for example, *the sky is a blanket of stars.*

mystic – one who has gone beyond the realm of duality to cognize the Universe in all its diversity as unification/One. The mystic lives in harmony with the Universe, and the Universe responds in kind.

Presence – used interchangeably with Divine Presence. One's Presence is an indicator of one's ability to be conscious or remain conscious.

Present – being and vibrating with the energy of Divinity, and exhibiting conscious awareness of that. It's more than just showing up for class.

quantum – a modern term used to describe the minutest of particles in the material realm of the Universe. Used in quantum mechanics, quantum science, quantum physics, quantum Universe, quantum field, quantum pool – all relating to what was once thought by the Newtonian scientific method as being a void, but has now been discovered to be filled with minute particles of intelligence. Ancient and modern rishis have been aware of such intelligence from time immemorial.

rishi – Sanskrit term for an enlightened individual who can see the minutest workings of the Universe.

sangha – a group of likeminded people coming together for devotion, as part of their devotional practice.

self – egoic personality involved in identification with objects, personalities, and situations outside of one's true identity.

Self (Cosmic Self) – pure consciousness beyond ego, beyond objects, experienced as Truth, Divinity, Supreme Presence. One's consciousness of one's Divine awareness beyond ego. Divinity expressing itself as Self.

shaman – Mongolian term that refers to one who sees things in Nature outside of the realm of normal vision, who understands the workings of elemental forces, and who is in touch with other dimensional realities. Similar references are medicine woman, medicine man, wizard.

stream of consciousness – as used in *The Isle of Is,* the term refers to that field or stream that connects the many different perceptions of Divinity – unconsciousness, awareness, and cosmic awareness.

synchronicity – Carl Jung's term to define an event or series of events that bring with them acknowledgement from Spirit or the Divine. Synchronous events appear to be coincidences (happenstance), but they are actually evidence of the workings of the Divine.

About the Isle of Is:
A Legend Unfolds

The Narrator

The narrator refers to him or herself as "we" because the word "I" solidifies the ego, whereas the word "we" removes us from the egoic bond. In addition, the narrator, and hence the reader, will come to understand that they are the Cosmic Self, which includes everyone and everything.

The Quotes

All quotes are in the voice of the ferryman, hence the use of "ye" instead of "you." We use the word "ye" because it also helps remove us from identification with the ego. Quotes for Chapters 2, 6 (Captain of the Boat E. Satva), 7, 8, 9, and 11 are our own, based on wisdom referenced throughout the book. The quote for Chapter 11 is paraphrased from the messages of Buddha, Christ, Krishna, Lao Tse Tung, and other spiritual masters with the knowledge of Truth.

The Stories

The experiences of the authors and of individuals in their meditation groups and retreats are the source material for the stories in *The Isle of Is*, including the appearance of the gnomes and the bird that wore hiking boots. Exceptions are the swami story, paraphrased from Swami Kripalvananda about himself as a younger man; the incident in which the woman saved her baby, which appeared in U.S. newspaper accounts in the 1950s; and the story of God trying to assist Ben during the flood, for which we do not know the origin.

The Isle of Is Experience

You can experience the Isle of Is on the sacred island of Koro in the Fiji Islands, where Caroline Cottom and Thom Cronkhite lead 'Isle of Is' and 'Awakening' retreats throughout the year. Former participants describe this experience as profound and life-changing.

You can also participate in an online group hosted by Thom and Caroline, to experience the book alongside other travelers. The online process provides personal contact with the authors, as well as a structure and time frame for reading and experiencing *The Isle of Is.*

For further information, contact Caroline and Thom: centerwithin@connect. com.fj or see their website: www.thecenterwithin.com

Isle of Is Groups

Meditation in the Ever-Present, Meditation with Divine Personalities, and Presence Practice are transformative. The more you engage with these and other aspects of the book, the more transformation you will experience. Doing the meditations with others will magnify the power exponentially.

Forming an Isle of Is group to read the book, meditate together, and share experiences is an ideal way to visit the Isle of Is. For suggested group guidelines, contact Caroline and Thom at: centerwithin@connect.com.fj

The group experience can also be combined with online support from the authors.

To Order *The Isle of Is* (book), the Meditation CD, and Visionary Art

If you would like to order additional copies of *The Isle of Is* or the Meditation CD, contact The Center Within at: centerwithin@connect.com.fj or 679-992-7204 in Fiji.

To see more of Jeff Bedrick's art, you can visit his website at: http://jeffreykbedrick. com

Chapter References

Most references for *The Isle of Is* have ancient roots. Original source material illuminates many of the concepts we discuss, while modern-day writers provide insights and additional information that today's readers and listeners may find more accessible. We recommend the resources listed below, both ancient and modern.

Opening to Timeless Truth
David Hawkins' "Map of Consciousness" and discussion of integrity are found in his books, *Power versus Force: An Anatomy of Consciousness* (1995) and *The Eye of the I: From Which Nothing Is Hidden* (Veritas Publishing, West Sedona, Arizona, 2001).

The writings of Jelaluddin Rumi, Sufi poet, can be found in *The Essential Rumi* (Castle Books, San Francisco, 1997).

The essence of the Agamas is found in *The Collected Works of Ramana Maharshi*, edited by Arthur Osborne (Samuel Weiser, Inc, York Beach, Maine, 1997).

For a discussion of ancient predictions about the era of spiritual opening in which we now find ourselves, see *The Holy Science* by Sri Yuteshwara, published by Self-Realization Fellowship. Also see Peruvian prophecies from the legend of Pachacuti.

Eckhart Tolle is a modern-day spiritual teacher whose writings about awakening to the Now have reached a worldwide audience. See *The Power of Now* (New World Library, Novato, California, 1999, and more recently, Namaste Publishing, Vancouver).

Cellular biologist Bruce Lipton and Psych-K founder Rob Williams discuss research showing that our perceptions, not our genes, determine our biology. See their videotape, "The Biology of Perception, The Psychology of Change" (2000).

Neuroscientist Candace Pert discusses the impact of our emotions on our bodies and our health on the audiotape, "Your Body Is Your Subconscious Mind" (2000).

Linguist George Lakoff and philosopher Mark Johnson describe the relationship between metaphors and human thought in their paradigm-shifting books, *Metaphors We Live By* (University of Chicago Press, 1980); and *Philosophy in the Flesh: The Embodied Mind and Its Challenge to Western Thought* (Basic Books [Perseus Books Group], New York, 1999).

1. Ferry to Sacred Island

The concept of the ferryman is common in Buddhist teachings and appears in the popular story of the Buddha's life, *Siddhartha,* by Hermann Hesse (New Directions Publishing Corp., 1951, and more recent editions). Stories about the mythical island of Avalon also describe a ferryman who carries people across the lake only when called by someone with highly developed mystical powers.

2. The Gate of Gratitude

Our approach to gratitude has its roots in the teachings of Jesus ("love your enemies"), Krishna as he talks to Arjuna in the Bhagavad-Gita, and Buddha.

For teachings about communing with Nature, see the writings of St Francis of Assisi, who committed himself to living the life of Jesus, and Chief Seattle, leader of the Suquamish tribe of Native Americans who lived in the American Northwest.

Natalie Goldberg's *Writing Down the Bones* (Shambala, Boston & London, 1986) is the modern-day seminal work for freeing up one's writing.

3. The Pool of (Ac)Knowledge

For Hindus, looking in the pool reveals the Universe duplicated and magnified, a double blessing.

Influenced by the writings of Madame Plavatsky, who brought the sacred knowledge of India and the East to Western Europe, Carl Jung coined the term "synchronicity" to describe those events that concur in time and space.

Acknowledging the Self as Divine is a concept found in the ancient Indian text, the Agamas, where Shiva tells his spouse Parvati that the most effective method of Self-realization is to acknowledge one's Self as Divine. Col. James Churchward references this concept dating back 70,000 years ago, as found on ancient tablets from the Pacific civilization of Mu (*The Children of Mu,* first published 1931; republished by BE Books & The C.W. Daniel Company Ltd., Albuquerque NM, 1988).

4. The Briar of Beliefs

Hinduism describes the world as Maya (delusion). Sufism teaches that God is Love, and anything outside of that is the briar. In Tibetan and other forms of Buddhism, the world is samsara (delusion); all is without form, without substance; the only thing that is, is Presence. Jesus taught that the kingdom of God is within (i.e., not in the briar of the world).

5. The Ever-Present

Many Westerners were introduced to Hindu and Buddhist concepts of Presence and Being by Maharishi Mahesh Yogi and Ram Dass (aka Richard Alpert) in the late 1960s and early 1970s. See Maharishi's *The Science of Being and the Art of Living* (Signet Books, NY, 1963) and Ram Dass's *Be Here Now* (Lama Foundation, Albuquerque, NM, 1971) and *The Only Dance There Is* (First Anchor Books, Random House, NY, 1974).

Eckhart Tolle's *The Power of Now* is a powerful, accessible approach to living in the Present (see reference under Preface, above).

Lynne McTaggart's *The Field* (HarperCollins Publishers, London, 2001) provides a synthesis of scientific discoveries of the 20th century that support the notion of an Ever-Present. For example, quantum mechanics, beginning with the work of Albert Einstein, is demonstrating that there is no such thing as a vacuum, that quantum fields are mediated by an exchange of energy, and that the real currency of the Universe – the very reason for its stability – is this exchange of energy. Science is beginning to catch up with ancient religious thought.

6. The Waves of Energy

An understanding that everything is made up of energy is prevalent throughout the cultures of Asia (e.g., Korea, Japan, China, Tibet, India). Buddhism and Hinduism, for example, identify energy as the essence of what makes up the body and the Universe, explaining the connection between the individual and the Universe. The earliest known documentation of this concept is approximately 35,000 years ago, when the Naacals (Nagas) of ancient India, predecessors of the Hindu empire, based an entire cosmology on the movement of energy, from the dream of God.

Meister Eckhardt's understanding of the Holy Grail is that the grail is Christ. The search for the grail (i.e., the human's spiritual search) is a quest for the highest vibration, in order to raise one's consciousness to that of Christ.

Japanese scientist Masaru Emoto's *Messages from Water* (I.H.M. General Research Institute, HADO Kyoikusha Co., Ltd.,) presents ground-breaking research on the impact of our thoughts and feelings on the cellular structure of water – an example of an exchange of energy (thought energy affecting the energy inherent in matter), with profound implications for how and what we think.

7. The Ocean of Being

The concept of Being is found in basic Vedic, Hindu, and Buddhist thought.

The white fish represents the living God: white symbolizes the Holy Spirit, and the fish symbolizes the Christ. The fish is the personification of God within the Ocean of Being.

Robert Frost's poem "Devotion" is found in *The Poetry of Robert Frost: The Collected Poems, Complete and Unabridged,* edited by Edward Connery Lathem (Henry Holt, 1969).

8. The Forest of Forgetfulness

Presence Practice is our version of an ancient Asian technique for dealing with physical sensations of pain and discomfort. A similar process called the WAVE is taught at Kripalu Center for Health and Well-Being, Lenox, Massachusetts.

The Divine Mother brings us back to the place of remembering who we really are. Examples of the Divine Mother are St. Bernadette, Mother Mary, Mother Teresa, and the Goddess as worshipped in religions that preceded the advent of Judaism, Christianity, Islam, and other male-dominated religions. Those who have written in depth about the Divine Mother and the Goddess religions include Marija Gimbutas *(The Language of the Goddess,* HarperCollins, New York, 1989), Rianne Eisler *(The Chalice and the Blade: Our History, Our Future,* HarperSanFrancisco, 1988), Joseph Campbell, and Krishananda, a Vedanta Society based in California.

9. Mount Metaphor

Our work on metaphors was stimulated in part by the writings of George Lakoff and Mark Johnson (see reference under Preface, above). Ancient practices related to "you are what you believe" include mantra meditation and contemplation, as clarified by Patanjali. See *The Yoga Sutra of Patanjali: Commentary on the Raja Yoga Sutra* by Sri Swami Satchidananda (Integral Yoga Publications, 1990).

For a study of the concept of karma, see the *Karma Mimasa,* an ancient Indian text.

10. Cascades of Compassion & Drops of Devotion

The ideas expressed about compassion and devotion are largely our own and result from our observation that one flows love and compassion much more powerfully to others if one is, first of all, compassionate toward and devoted to one's Divine Self.

11. The Stream of Consciousness

The ideas about the Stream of Consciousness come from scientific evidence that everything is connected, everything is energy, and energy is energy. See the work of Nikola Tessla, Albert Einstein, and numerous other scientists of the past 70 years.

Our personification of Mother Earth is based on the Gaia concept that there is consciousness in the Earth, which is a living organism. Thomas Banyacya, Hopi interpreter, expresses the Hopi perspective: "The Earth is a living growing person, and all things on it are her children."

Two resources that assist one in listening to the body are *The Self-Health Guide: a Personal Program for Holistic Living* (Kripalu Publications, Box 793, Lenox, Massachusetts, USA, 1980); and *Perfect Health: the Complete Mind/Body Guide,* Deepak Chopra, M.D. (Harmony Books, New York, 1991). Both have roots in the ancient Indian health system called Ayurveda.

Many generations of Aztec, Druidic, Hawaiian, Incan, Maori, Saskatchewan, and other indigenous peoples have used water for healing.

The fairy folk are named after deities of various cultures: Angus Mac Og, Irish god of youth, love, and beauty; Ceres, Roman goddess of agriculture; Dakuwangga, Fijian sea god enshrined in a tattooed shark that inhabited the Koro Sea; Devi, Hindu goddess of fertility, rain, health, and Nature; Gyffes, Celtic god of light, "a bright lion with a sure hand"; Haumea, Hawaiian-personified Mother Earth through whom flows the Spirit of the Earth, who can create fish or fruit on the tree; and Papatuanuku, Maori Earth Mother.

12. Tides of Truth

The Upanishads, Rig Veda, and Bhagavad-Gita are the sources of ideas about the Cosmic Self. See especially *Maharishi Mahesh Yogi on the Bhagavad-Gita: A New Translation and Commentary,* Chapters 1-6 (Penguin Books, London, 1969).

The concept of following the silver thread of Truth is found in George MacDonald's fairytale *The Princess and the Goblin,* first published circa 1882. Penguin Books Ltd re-published MacDonald's fairytales in 1964.

13. The Constant Cosmos of Is

A magnificent cosmos awaits you. Go outside of your home, town, or city and look up at the sky.

About the Authors

Thom Cronkhite

Thom Cronkhite is a medical intuitive and vibrational energy healer who lives in a state of awakenness. He is able to perceive an individual's state of health or disease – mental, emotional, spiritual and physical – and once blockages are recognized, to facilitate their removal energetically. Apparently born "awakened," he experiences life as constant joy and peace, fully in the present.

To understand how his perceptions and experiences fit into the world, Thom studied art and ancient religions at the University of Texas, which led him to delve deeply into ancient sacred texts, meditation practices, and quantum mechanics. Later he engaged in advanced studies in electron theory, which gave him a platform to communicate with others about his understanding of the workings of the Universe. For two decades he worked as a master electrician, business owner, energy consultant, and liaison between local government and the construction industry.

Thom has discovered that his healing work is similar to that of many indigenous healing cultures. Maori tohunga (shamans), Chinese Qi Gong Grandmasters, and Vedic vibrational healers from India recognize Thom's ability to move and purify the physical energy that exists in and around the human body and beyond.

Caroline Cottom

Caroline Cottom is recognized for her ability to impart her spiritual gifts and awareness in a wide range of settings, from spiritual and meditation retreats, to meetings with political leaders in the former Soviet Union and the halls of Congress. In her roles as a writer, teacher, coalition builder, and seminar leader, she has influenced the U.S. creative arts, education, and political spheres for more than 25 years. She has also consulted with the Fiji government to bring clarity, insight, and inspiration to their work with the youth of that country, and with large corporations such as Dupont.

Caroline is the published author of numerous articles, essays, short stories, and poetry, and a former faculty member at Vanderbilt University and Watkins College of Art&Design. In these environments she taught courses on creativity and designed curriculum and professional development for public school teachers.

Former Director of the Nuclear Weapons Freeze Campaign and the U.S. Comprehensive Test Ban (CTB) Coalition, Caroline bridged politics and spirituality, bringing values of love, respect, and community into an arena known for its competitiveness and divisiveness. The CTB coalition of 75 national organizations that she created brought an end to U.S. nuclear testing in 1992. As a grassroots lobbyist and organizer, she developed networks that involved dozens of states and hundreds of local communities. She also co-led the global effort to amend the Partial Test Ban Treaty to prohibit underground testing.

Caroline has led hundreds of seminars and workshops at national conferences in the arts, education, political/social change, and spirituality.

Together, Thom and Caroline lead spiritual retreats in Fiji, New Zealand, and the United States, teaching others how to live a life of profound peace and joy. Using approaches unique to their work, they assist others to feel energy and understand their connection to Divinity. They also conduct online courses based on their teachings.